Mandate of Heaven

TREASURES FROM
CHINA'S IMPERIAL DYNASTIES

by Barry Till

Hongkong Bank of Canada

加拿大滙豐銀行

Member HSBC *Group*

滙豐集團成員

ART GALLERY OF GREATER VICTORIA

1996

Canadian Cataloguing in Publication Data

Till, Barry.
  Mandate of Heaven

  Includes bibliographical references.
  Catalogue of an exhibition held at the Art Gallery of Greater
  Victoria
  ISBN 0-88885-151-0

  1. Art, Chinese – Exhibitions. 2. Art Gallery of Greater
Victoria – Exhibitions. I. Art Gallery of Greater Victoria. II.
Title.
  N7342.T55 1996   709.'51'07471128   C96-910423-5

This exhibition and publication has been funded by
Hongkong Bank of Canada.

Published by
ART GALLERY OF GREATER VICTORIA
1040 Moss Street, Victoria
British Columbia, Canada V8V 4P1

Designed and printed by
MORRISS PRINTING COMPANY LTD.
1745 Blanshard Street
Victoria, B.C., Canada

Contents

ACKNOWLEDGEMENTS

*W*e are very grateful to Hongkong Bank of Canada for generously sponsoring this exhibition and catalogue and especially to David Bond, Vice-president of Government and Public Affairs, for his enthusiastic support. It gives the Art Gallery of Greater Victoria an opportunity to publish its Chinese art collection as a whole for the first time. The collection is truly a significant one, though weak in a few fields, namely, early Chinese bronzes, certain ceramics and cloisonné. Therefore, we have chosen to borrow a few choice pieces from private collectors to fill in some of these gaps. We would like to thank lenders for these loans and the donors of the past who have generously given Chinese works of art to the Art Gallery of Greater Victoria making it the rich resource it is.

The Art Gallery of Greater Victoria collection of Chinese art is of a type and quality to interest the serious collector as well as the general public. In many instances, there are outstanding treasures of which international scholars may be pleased to learn.

The assistance of the following staff members has been vital to the success of the exhibition: Mary and Brian Patten, Chris Russell and Ann Tighe. Special thanks must go to Jean Addison for her role in the project. We are deeply grateful to Jamie Drouin for the colour photography and some of the black and white photography; to Paula Swart for proofreading and to Martha E. Cooke for her wonderful job of editing.

Barry Till
Curator of Asian Art, June 1996

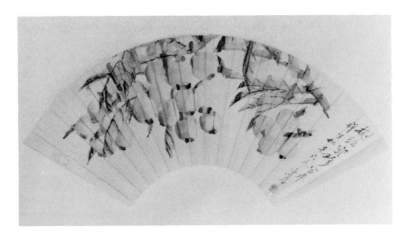

Xu Gu (1834-1896)
Gems on the Tree
Fan painting; ink and colours on paper
Gift of Brian S. McElney
AGGV

*I*t was fifty-two years ago, in 1944, that the Art Gallery of Greater Victoria presented its first exhibitions, one of which in that founding year was an exhibition of Chinese art borrowed from the Smithsonian Institute in Washington DC. At that time the Gallery had no permanent collection, in fact it had no permanent home. Rather, the initial interest in Asian art as a focal point for the fledgling Art Gallery was made known to all in the show room of an automobile sales company. The Gallery began its collection in 1951, having found a permanent home, with the first works of Asian art being acquired in that first year of collecting activity. The activity in the collecting, presenting and publishing of Asian art has been an integral part of the Gallery's endeavours since the outset, and the interest and commitment to this aspect of the Gallery's work has been supported by individuals and business over the years, those across Canada and those beyond our national borders.

It is with great pleasure that we present *Mandate of Heaven: Treasures from China's Imperial Dynasties*, and we are particularly grateful to Hongkong Bank of Canada for their generous support of this exhibition and publication, and to the presentations in both Victoria and Vancouver. The Art Gallery of Greater Victoria's collection of Chinese art is truly a Canadian treasure. Representing one of the oldest civilizations in the world, it gives us an opportunity to understand the roots of so many newer world civilizations, including our own. Its timing is opportune – the British Columbia Government is now initiating new curriculum in Asia civilizations, and what better way to study the riches of the East than by seeing them! Through this exhibition the Art Gallery of Greater Victoria is pleased to make these collections accessible and we hope this publication and exhibition will provide a basis both for the new curriculum and for increased pubic interest and knowledge by audiences of all ages and backgrounds.

Hongkong Bank of Canada by joining us has made this public access possible, as they did when they joined us on a similar venture ten years ago with their support of our *Chinese Jade: Stone for the Emperors*. That exhibition and publication likewise travelled to several centres in Canada. I would again like to thank Hongkong Bank, and William Dalton, President , and David Bond, Vice-president of Government and Public Affairs, for their commitment, interest and support. Our partnership with the Bank over the years has been of significant assistance to us as we stretch across the Pacific and enrich the understanding of East and West.

I would also like to add my thanks to those of Curator Barry Till to the donors who have made our collection what it is, and to the lenders who generously have loaned works for this exhibition to fill in the areas where we are still weak in our representation. To Barry Till go my special thanks for all his work in developing the collection and in presenting, organizing and producing this special project. I wish to thank all the staff who have assisted him in this work, as it was only became a reality with that collective effort.

It is my hope that you enjoy this publication and exhibition, and that the treasures presented here will become special landmarks for you.

Patricia E. Bovey
Director, AGGV, July 1996

*H*ongkong Bank of Canada takes great pride in funding *Mandate of Heaven*, the special exhibition of the Chinese treasures from the Art Gallery of Greater Victoria collection.

This Gallery's collection, one of the best in Canada, is a national treasure which has received too little exposure. The exhibition is aimed at giving a wider audience the opportunity to marvel at the artistic wonders of one of the world's oldest and richest cultures.

Positioned as it is on the rim of the Pacific, British Columbia has developed increasingly important and extensive relations with Asia and most particularly China. Our commerce is steadily increasing and now we are fortunate to have sizable cultural and family ties that unite us in an even closer common destiny.

What better way to improve our understanding of the region, the culture and the people than to enjoy these masterpieces? Each has a story to tell and each provides us with a perspective on a diverse and rich culture. Collectively they tell us much and hopefully make those living in or visiting British Columbia aware of the Art Gallery of Greater Victoria . . . a significant treasure.

William Dalton
President and CEO

Hongkong Bank of Canada
加拿大滙豐銀行
Member HSBC Group
滙豐集團成員

*V*ictoria is an important city on the Asia Pacific rim. It is Canada's furthest city to the west and is the nearest Canadian city to the Far East. The city has played a pivotal role in early exchanges between Canada and Asia. It seems only fitting that Victoria's gallery, the Art Gallery of Greater Victoria (AGGV), would have one of the most distinguished Far Eastern art collections in Canada.

It's Asian art collections, acquired over the past five decades, and travelling exhibitions have become quite well-known throughout Canada. The extensive Chinese art collection of the Gallery, encompassing various media and all periods of Chinese art, is extremely varied. Some artifacts are internationally known for their rarity and significance. Several of them have been borrowed for exhibitions and published in scholarly journals and books throughout the world. A large number of people have generously donated Chinese art and supported Chinese exhibitions over the past few decades. Regretfully, we cannot acknowledge each and every one, but will try to mention the most significant donors to the Chinese collection.

The first large donation of Chinese artifacts to the AGGV came in 1972 from the Chen King Foh family who had moved to Canada from Indonesia. They gave a sizable number of Chinese ceramics and textiles. A second important early donor of Chinese works of art was the late Mrs. Isabel Pollard of San Francisco, who gave valuable paintings and some jade and ceramic artifacts. She is best known, however, for her considerable donation of Japanese works of art to the AGGV. The Chinese art collection has been growing steadily over the last decade and has received major donations of ceramics, bronzes and paintings from three major sources: Mr. and Mrs. R. W. Finlayson, the Rev. Dr. James M. Menzies family and Brian S. McElney.

The late Mr. R. W. Finlayson, a Toronto entrepreneur and patron of the arts, and his wife, Marjorie, donated extremely important Chinese works of art to the AGGV. In addition, they gave an impressive collection of Japanese paintings. In the last decade, Mrs. Marjorie Finlayson has graciously donated a number of important Chinese artifacts including paintings, tomb figurines and an enormous stone Buddha head. *Lotus*, a superb Chinese scroll painting donated by her in 1988, is considered to be an outstanding work by the renowned artist, Dao Ji (1641 – 1714) and it is the most widely published Chinese scroll in Canada.

The late Rev. Dr. James M. Menzies (1885 – 1957) and his family lived in China in the 1910s, 1920s and 1930s. Rev. Menzies was a Presbyterian missionary who had a keen interest in Chinese archaeology, especially in "oracle bones." He eventually received a Ph.D. degree in Chinese studies and joined the Royal Ontario Museum. Following his death in 1957, his family inherited his personal collection. Each family member has generously loaned artifacts for exhibitions and has donated important works of art to the AGGV. His son and former Canadian Ambassador to China, Arthur R. Menzies, donated extremely rare painting and calligraphy scrolls from the Tang dynasty (618 – 907); his daughter, Frances Menzies Newcombe, donated several fine Tang and Song ceramics; and his daughter, Marion Menzies Hummel, and her son, James Menzies Hummel, donated some beautiful early bronze and ceramic artifacts.

Brian S. McElney, a former lawyer in Hong Kong and now Honorary Curator at the Museum of East Asian Art in Bath, England, has been a major lender and donor to the

AGGV for more than two decades. He has donated the largest number of Chinese works of all collectors to the AGGV, including Chinese bronzes, jades and ceramics from the Shang dynasty (16th–11th century BC) through to the Qing dynasty (1644–1911). He has donated some very important Chinese tomb figurines as well as a large number of important, contemporary, Chinese paintings of which only a few examples are included in this publication.

Other notable contributors to the Chinese collection are the late Mrs. Sheila Anderson (ceramics of the Six Dynasties period, 220–589); Mrs. Renée Chipman (late 17th century Kesi tapestries); Mr. Ernie A. Davis of Calgary (a rare set of late 17th century Chinese Buddhist Hell scrolls); Sir James Howard Thornton memorial gifts (cloisonné and jade artifacts); Mrs. Carol Potter Peckham of San Francisco (an extensive collection of Chinese Yixing teapots); Mrs. Helen Sawyer of Victoria (a large collection of snuff bottles); Mr. Syd Hoare of Kelowna (a fine collection of Chinese ceramics); and recently, Mr. Irving Zucker of Hamilton (important Chinese ceramics and tomb figurines).

As we can see from this brief summary, the Chinese art collection has had dedicated and enlightened donors and is enjoying a steady growth of important artifacts. Without all these generous patrons of the past and present, the Chinese art collection would not be what it is today. We are deeply indebted to our donors for their discriminating taste and foresight. It is amazing that such an important Chinese collection could be assembled almost entirely through donation with only an extremely small number of artifacts coming through purchases. Colin Graham, the first director of the Gallery, started the ball rolling by encouraging the establishment of an Asian art collection and subsequent directors continued to support its growth enthusiastically. Today it is one of the finest Asian art collections in Canada.

The Asian department of the AGGV also receives much moral support from the Asian Art Society of Victoria and its long-time president, Hilda Hale. They have been hosting monthly lectures at the AGGV on Asian subjects for more than a decade. The dedicated and talented AGGV staff members have assisted in innumerable ways over the years, including cataloguing, preserving and exhibiting this rich heritage.

The first gallery space to be devoted exclusively to Asian art was the Fred and Isabel Pollard Gallery, which was formally opened as part of a new wing at the Gallery on October 4, 1977. Since then, the AGGV has enjoyed sharing its Asian art collection with the rest of Canada. In the last two decades, the AGGV has organized about a dozen national tours of Asian art exhibitions, drawn to a large extent from the Gallery's collection and each with an accompanying publication, many of which were in several languages. In all, the Gallery has more than forty Asian art publications to its credit. Numerous venues throughout British Columbia for the AGGV Asian shows have also been arranged, giving the public wide access to these treasures. Together, these initiatives highlighting Asian art underline the AGGV's leadership nationally in the field of Asian art.

At home, the AGGV mounts between ten and twelve Asian art exhibitions annually, each representing various aspects and geographic regions of Asian art creation. These are presented on a rotating basis. Unfortunately, due to limited space, the AGGV does not as yet have ongoing permanent exhibitions, running concurrently with the special shorter term exhibits. As the AGGV is currently engaged in planning a new facility, we are looking forward to having several galleries dedicated exclusively to the permanent display of our most significant Asian treasures, as well as space for the rotating specialized shows. This of course, is in addition to those areas for other aspects of the Gallery's programme, and to those dedicated to research and resources. Our collection of Asian art published here will of course be a focal point of the new Gallery.

Ancient Chinese scholars held that the virtue of the rulers was inextricably related to the successful rise to power or the ultimate failure of each ruling dynasty. The sovereign who came to be known as the "Son of Heaven" was confirmed by Heaven as the legitimate leader of mankind and the sole intermediary in negotiating with Heaven. It was believed that Heaven was an all-powerful, impersonal deity or force that governed the workings of the universe. The idea developed that Heaven would befriend the righteous and benevolent ruler to maintain harmony on earth, but would withdraw its support for an evil ruler who had forsaken virtue. Thus, this "Mandate of Heaven" was not a divine right, irrevocable or eternal. It was generally believed that the Mandate of Heaven doctrine served as a powerful moral restraint on the ruling family, who came to believe the reward of moral virtue was prosperity, while the penalty for not maintaining the correct standards of morality was disaster. The concept also offered the justification for power for the successful rebel while the unsuccessful rebels were condemned as villains. There is an old Chinese proverb:

He who succeeds becomes Emperor,
he who fails is a bandit.

The concept of winning or losing the Mandate of Heaven would persist each time an imperial regime was replaced by another throughout China's long dynastic history. The death knell of a dynastic house, thought to be an act of Heaven, was often signalled by eclipses of the sun, rebellions, and natural calamities such as earthquakes, floods, droughts, famines and plagues For the first appearance of the concept known as the "Mandate of Heaven" see the section on the Zhou dynasty.

Paleolithic Cultures

Archaeological excavations of this century have revealed that China holds an important position in the development of early mankind. An abundance of recently excavated human fossils and artifacts such as primitive tools and weapons from Paleolithic cultures have resulted in the reassessing of China's prehistoric period.

Traces of early pre-human animals called hominids appear at sites scattered sparsely throughout China. The most ancient hominid fossils yet to be found in China belong to the Xihoudu culture of Shanxi province and the Yuanmou culture of Hunan province, which could be more than a million years old. Excavated material of primitive man from the Kehe culture of Shanxi and the Lantian culture of Shanxi have been found to date as far back as 500,000 to 600,000 years ago. The best known primitive culture of China is that of Peking man in the Beijing area, who lived some 400,000 to 500,000 years ago.

Neolithic Cultures   *c.* 8000 – 21st century BC

Neolithic cultures settled over a wide area along river valleys and small basins in North China, that is, primarily along the Yellow River and its tributaries and south to the Yangzi River. Hunting and fishing became secondary for these cultures after they settled down. They lived in villages of stamped earth structures, cultivated millet, and domesticated animals such as pigs, dogs, sheep, cattle and chickens. The invention of ceramic containers enabled them to store water and food as well as to cook meals. They made crude stone and bone implements such as grinding stones, scrapers, axes, chisels, and sickles, and ornaments of jade and stone. They domesticated silkworms and may have developed a loom for weaving. They seem to have had a belief in the afterlife as indicated by the ornaments, the utensils and stored foods which were buried with the dead.

Hundreds of archaeological excavations have revealed that there were basically two well-established cultures with regional variations during China's Neolithic period: the Painted Pottery or Yangshao Culture (late 6th millennium to 3rd millennium BC) and the Black Pottery or Longshan Culture (3rd millennium BC).

The earliest of the two, the Yangshao Culture, was found along the central plains connecting to the northwest province of Gansu. Their farming villages, which were fairly large, show that they sometimes shifted settlements, but with repetitive reoccupations. These villages were inhabited by members of clans and lineages. There appears to have been no stratification of social classes in their society.

They made two qualities of pottery vessels: utilitarian pots of impressed, gray earthenware made with either cord or mat-basket and fine pots of red earthenware painted in slip colours of black, red, and white in abstract and geometric designs. The latter are amongst the most beautiful ceramics ever produced by a Neolithic culture. These pots were made by coiling strips of clay without the use of a potter's wheel.

The Yangshao Culture was followed by and, in some cases, was contemporary with the Longshan Culture. In the beginning, the Longshan Culture from the east and northeast penetrated the central plain area, but not the northwest region where the Yangshao Culture continued for a time longer and is known as the Gansu Yangshao Culture. In contrast to the Yangshao Culture, the Longshan Culture had relatively permanent settlements defended by walls of stamped earth. With them we find the first signs of religious ancestor worship. The Longshan Culture improved upon agriculture and animal husbandry and highly specialized craftsmen began to emerge. One of the biggest differences between the Longshan and Yangshao Cultures was their ceramic objects. The Longshan produced fine burnished black pottery which was very thin due to being thrown on a rapidly turning potter's wheel. The technical standard of control and experimentation was far in advance of Yangshao pottery. The shapes of these new wares were varied and many of the types were passed on to the metal vessels of the succeeding Bronze Age.

A culture with Longshan features, known as Liangzhu (c. 3300 – 2250 BC) in Zheijiang province produced a large number of well-crafted jade artifacts. They had a variety of shapes such as the *bi* (disc), the *cong* (tubular object) and other ornaments which were forerunners of the jade carvings of the succeeding Shang dynasty.

Xia Dynasty   21st – 16th century BC

The primitive Neolithic cultures appear to have evolved into a feudal society around the 21st century BC. According to early Chinese records, a kingdom known as the Xia was established sometime before the Shang dynasty. This kingdom covered vast areas along the Yellow River and was run by a system of hereditary monarchs. This period seems to show the first signs of an emerging civilization in China. The Xia had city walls with moats, their own army and a penal code. They knew about sericulture, the wheel, and the casting of bronze. Evidence excavated at the Erlitou site in Yanshi, Henan province, also shows that China appears to have entered the Bronze Age late in the Xia period.

Shang Dynasty   16th – 11th century BC

In the 16th century BC, the Xia dynasty was overthrown by the Shang or Yin dynasty. The Shang conquest of the Xia did not mark any sharp break in the emerging culture of China, and the territory continued to be ruled over by hereditary chiefs called kings who were succeeded on death by either their brothers or sons.

The Shang nation, which was located in the central and lower plains of the Yellow River, was a limited domain made up of city-states with nearby settlements that regularly presented tribute. The cities were not large and were surrounded by earthen ramparts for protection. The economy was based mainly on agriculture and animal husbandry with some hunting and fishing. Despite primitive tools of bone, wood and stone, there was a sufficient output of agricultural products to meet the demands of the population.

Shang civilization was characterized by a strong centralized government and was organized along feudal lines with two distinct classes, the warrior nobility and the commoners. The wide gap between ruler and ruled is illustrated by excavated Shang sites which show that palace buildings were large and imposing, while common people lived in semi-subterranean, crude, pit dwellings built of wood and tamped earth. The rulers had a sizable army with chariots and war with nearby neighbours was a means of increasing their wealth. There are records which mention campaigns using as many as 3,000, 5,000 and 13,000 troops.

Both bronze and jade objects were highly prized by the Shang ruling class, who monopolized their manufacture. Bronze weapons were a source of power for the Shang aristocracy over the masses, while bronze ritual vessels and jade ceremonial objects were venerated as symbols for elaborate ceremonies and psychological support necessary for their political dominance over the rest of the population. The rulers maintained authority through religion and thus legitimized their reason for being in power. The religion comprised of ceremonies related to the fertility cult and ancestor worship became a way of life at this time. The kings made lavish sacrifices to propitiate *Shang Di*, the Supreme Ancestor, in hope of gaining favours for the nation, such as abundant harvests and successful battles. They also acted as mediator between the people and the spirits and were able to placate fate and to influence natural phenomena through rituals.

Divination by use of "oracle bones" was part of the complex rituals of the Shang dynasty. This foretelling of the future by cracks on heated bones and turtle shells appears to have been inherited from the earlier Longshan and Xia Cultures. The earliest examples of written Chinese appear for the first time on the oracle bones used in the divination rites of the Shang dynasty. A question was inscribed on a bone or shell and the answer was sought by means of cracking the bone through heating with fire. The cracks would then be read by a diviner who would thereby control much power. The questions and the answers that were inscribed on the bones were related to sacrifices, agriculture, the weather, journeys, war and hunting.

The ruling class of the Shang paid a great deal of attention to the burial of their dead. Human and animal sacrifices were practised on a colossal scale at the monumental tombs of the nobility. It is estimated that at one excavated late Shang tomb there were three hundred or more sacrificed victims. It was believed that these sacrificed people would serve the master in the afterlife as they had done while they were alive. It was also customary to consign hundreds of articles, both of use and value such as bronze and jade items, to accompany the royal corpse to the spirit world.

Zhou Dynasty   11th–3rd century BC

The Shang dynasty was involved in exhaustive military encounters with rivals in the southwestern part of China. This may have weakened them enough to allow a people in the west, later known as the Zhou, to defeat the Shang in the 11th century BC and establish themselves as the new rulers of what was then China.

The Zhou were originally an organized group of pastoral people in the west who paid tribute to the Shang. The superior aspects of Shang civilization may have stimulated progressive changes in Zhou society ultimately impelling them to challenge the Shang for supremacy of central China. When the Zhou, who were a linear recipient of the Shang tradition, replaced the Shang as rulers, there was no major or immediate change in the culture.

In state religion, which was the basis of political power for the ruling line, the Zhou adopted a new concept. In contrast to *Shang Di* (the Supreme Ancestor) of the Shang, the Zhou developed the idea of *Tian*, meaning heaven, and each of the Zhou kings referred to himself as the "Son of Heaven." Thus, the Zhou rulers, who were both kings and priests, became mediators between man and the supreme heaven, and the controllers of the people's fate and welfare. They justified their conquest of the Shang and their authority over the rest of the population on the grounds that they had received the "Mandate of Heaven." This Mandate concept of legitimizing one's claim to the throne would carry on uninterruptedly throughout Chinese history, by both Chinese and non-Chinese dynasties, until the fall of the last imperial dynasty in 1911.

The Zhou continued the Shang use of bronze and jade ceremonial objects in their religious rituals. Their magnificent ceremonies were largely geared to the seasons and became increasingly complex. There were basically two types, one for divine benevolence and the other for ancestor worship. Evidence for the magnitude of their ceremonies has come down to us through their bronze ritual vessels and jade ceremonial objects, which have been excavated in great numbers by archaeologists in this century. Zhou bronze vessels often bear long inscriptions which supply information regarding the occasion of their manufacture.

It was during the early Zhou period that the concept of "Middle Kingdom" came into being. The Chinese were unaware of the great civilizations to the west and believed China to be the centre of the civilized world surrounded on all sides by "barbarians." Hence they referred to their country as *Zhong Guo* or Middle Kingdom, which is still the name the Chinese use to this day.

Following the conquest of the Shang, the Zhou greatly expanded their territory and this resulted in an accelerated growth of the society, economy and politics. The Zhou kings bestowed countless grants of land or fiefs on their relatives and allies and thus set up a rigid feudal hierarchy. Hereditary lords controlled these fiefs which became centres for state functions. They were expected to prevent rebellions and contribute revenue to the central authority at the Zhou capital, which was near the modern city of Xi'an.

For two and a half centuries the Zhou rulers had firm control over the dominion, as none of these fiefs was strong enough to challenge central authority. When the royal power and influence of the Zhou waned, the various states became virtually independent and in 771 BC, one feudal lord attacked the capital and murdered the king. The remainder of the royal court fled east and re-established the capital at Luoyang. The unity and the power of the central state, however, had vanished and the Zhou king became a mere figurehead. The period before 771 BC is known as the Western Zhou and, after the move of the capital to Luoyang, as the Eastern Zhou.

After 771 BC, the Zhou disintegrated into a number of small belligerent states, none of which was strong enough to assume undisputed leadership until the 3rd century BC. These independent states practised their own religious rites and created their own regional bronze casting industry to supply the necessary ritual vessels. This resulted in a wide variety of styles. As time went on, bronze vessels were used increasingly for secular purposes, such as banquets, symbols of prestige, tokens of good faith and dowries, rather than religious.

Eastern Zhou society was highly stratified between the wealthy aristocracy and the commoner. There was a high degree of specialization in the crafts and industries of this time. Markets and industrial quarters which in the past had been outside the city wall, now occurred within the large city enclosures of tamped earth. In farming at this time, the development of an iron metallurgy provided efficient iron implements to replace the stone and bone ones. This improvement in farm implements increased productivity and allowed the population to grow and expand into new areas. With a more sophisticated administration, the people were effectively organized to build large defensive walls along their borders. They constructed irrigation systems and roads thus enabling better communications and trade. This period gave rise to the introduction of metal currency to replace the barter system; an infantry, archers and also a cavalry to supersede chariots; and the use of cross-bows and iron swords.

The Eastern Zhou is considered an exciting and romantic age despite the seemingly endless chaos. It can be divided into two major periods: the Spring and Autumn period (771 – 475 BC) and the Warring States period (475 – 221 BC). An unparalleled explosion of intellectual activity took place during the Spring and Autumn period. Of special note is the development of Chinese philosophies including the mainstreams of Confucianism and Daoism. In contrast, an all-out sruggle between the various states for absolute supremacy occurred during the Warring States period and culminated in the unification of China under the Qin dynasty in 221 BC.

Qin   221 – 207 BC   *and Han*   206 BC – AD 220   *Dynasties*

By 221 BC, the powerful army of the Qin state had crushed all the other feudal states and united the country under one ruler who called himself Qin Shihuangdi, the First Emperor of Qin. The year 221 BC was a turning point in Chinese history, for it marked the beginning of the concept of a Chinese Empire with a single imperial authority. From the name Qin (Ch'in) came the name "China," which is used to this day. The first emperor set up an absolute, authoritarian rule; linked the various sections of defensive walls in the north into one "Great Wall" and took steps in the direction of cultural unification of all China by standardizing the written language, coinage, and weights and measures. He built himself a vast palace and an enormous tomb, parts of which have been excavated. Extremely well-modelled, life-size, terra cotta soldiers and horses, numbering in the thousands, have been uncovered as well as amazingly complicated bronze cast chariots. The artifacts thus far excavated from Qin sites have revealed the incredibly high level of artistic achievement of the craftsmen of the era.

Upon the death of the ruthless First Emperor in 210 BC, his incapable son succeeded him and the unpopular dynasty quickly fell apart plunging the country into civil war. A peasant rebel named Liu Bang was the ultimate victor of the civil war and founded the Han dynasty in 206 BC. Han China was remarkably prosperous and was one of the longest dynasties in Chinese history, lasting until AD 220. The dynasty was held in such high esteem by the Chinese that to this day they refer to themselves as the Han nationality.

The Han rulers restored aspects of the old feudal order and adopted a limited policy of *laissez-faire* in domestic matters. There were many innovations in agricultural techniques and military organization. The system of government and social structure established and developed by the Han rulers would remain basically the same for the next two thousand years until the overthrow of the last imperial dynasty in 1911. Their culture impacted on neighbouring countries such as Korea, Vietnam and Japan, and this sphere of influence would continue to exist for centuries.

The Han emperor, Wu (r. 140 – 87 BC), greatly expanded the Chinese empire and established a centralized government based on Confucian doctrine. The emperor called to his service outstanding scholars and men of ability and developed an enduring examination system to attract men of virtue and wisdom for his imperial government. Emperor Wu also sent missions into Central Asia to acquire Ferghanan horses which were ideal cavalry horses for fighting the troublesome Huns along China's border. These legendary horses were nicknamed "Heavenly Horses" for their speed and "Blood Sweating Horses" for when they galloped, parasites would fall off and blood would mix with the sweaty foam forming a pink colour. Because they played such a vital role in safeguarding and strengthening China, they were immortalized by Han sculptors and artists.

The Han dynasty was divided for a brief span from AD 8 to AD 23 when a usurper named Wang Mang briefly held power. Members of the imperial Han dynasty were able to restore power at Luoyang in the period known as Eastern Han until AD 220 when corruption at court and worsening financial problems ended the dynasty. Three generals proclaimed themselves emperor and divided China into "Three Kingdoms."

The Han dynasty brought China unprecedented economic development and international prestige. Art during the Han dynasty ceased both to be solely the prerogative of the emperors and nobles and to be made for purely religious purposes. Instead, secular interests to appeal to a wider circle of patrons took hold and thus art filtered down to more members of society. Wealthy families, now enjoying great affluence and access to exotic imported goods, became great patrons of the arts. Contact with Central Asia and the West resulted in the influence of foreign styles which greatly enriched China's art and cultural traditions. Four centuries of Han political unification saw the flowering of arts and crafts in China. All forms of art from jade and stone carvings to bronze, lacquer and ceramic artifacts as well as painting and calligraphy were injected with an incredible creative vitality. Archaeological finds of Han remains, which usually comes from tombs, testifies to the greatness and splendour of the period.

Six Dynasties 220 – 589

The period of strife and disunity following the breakup of the Han dynasty is referred to by Chinese scholars as the Six Dynasties period. The Six Dynasties period refers to Wu (222 – 280), Eastern Jin (317 – 420), Liu Song (420 – 479), Southern Qi (479 – 502), Liang (502 – 557) and Chen (557 – 589), all of which had their capital at present day Nanjing. Many Western scholars, including scholars at the British Museum, incorrectly exclude the Wu and include the Western Jin (265 – 316), with its capital at Luoyang, as one of the "Six Dynasties."

It was in some ways similar to the Dark Ages of European history. This era saw China with no strong centralized government, inadequate rulers and the country divided into numerous dynasties. Generally speaking the partition saw foreign or barbarian dynasties ruling in the north and native Chinese dynasties governing the south, with constant strife between them. It was a time when wealth and political power tended to be concentrated in the hands of regional warlords with huge private armies and large landholdings. During this period, tens of thousands of Chinese refugees fled from the north to the south.

In the north, the barbarian dynasties ruled over their own nomadic peoples as well as a sizable Chinese population. They were usually quickly assimilated, within a generation or two, by the civilizing aspects of Chinese culture and became Sinicized. The alien dynasties were greatly influenced by the Buddhist faith and its art coming from India through Central Asia. As a result, it was a time of great creative production in works of art, particularly in the field of monumental Buddhist stone sculptures and grotto wall murals. The most powerful, foreign dynasty in the north,which produced the most significant and outstanding works of art, was the Northern Wei dynasty (386 – 535) founded by a proto-Turkish people called Toba. Its figural images were noted for elegance, linear and angular rhythms, and elongation of form. This style showed Indian and Central Asian influences as well as Chinese aesthetic sensibilities. The Buddhist grottoes made during this era are stunningly beautiful.

The Chinese dynasties in the south carried on the same basic bureaucracy as the Han. The principal group with power was the wealthy, landowning aristocracy who supported Confucianism and Daoism and began embracing Buddhism. The most important of the Southern dynasties was the Liang Dynasty (502 – 557). The long reigning Liang emperor, Wu (r. 502 – 550), was the most significant ruler of the period. A devout Buddhist, he constructed countless temples which constituted a serious threat to the economic stability of the south.

The Southern Dynasties reigned amid luxuries and refinement at their capital of Nanjing, which was a brilliant centre of spiritual and aesthetic innovations. The Southern dynasties made impressive contributions in form and design to Chinese art, especially in the field of monumental stone tomb sculptures, Buddhist sculptural art, and high-fired stoneware with celadon-like glazes. Major innovations in refined painting by such masters as Gu Kaizhi and talented calligraphers such as Wang Xizhi set the standards for centuries to come.

Sui 581–618 *and Tang* 618–907 *Dynasties*

China was again unified in 589 by the founders of the Sui dynasty. While it did not hold the Mandate of Heaven for long, it did lay the groundwork for the prosperity to come. The short-lived dynasty had two strong emperors, Wen (r. 581–604) and Yang (r. 604– 618). Emperor Wen consolidated his empire by establishing a rigorous centralized government based on Confucian doctrines, and brought in revenue by using a tax structure based on the equal field system. Emperor Yang is most noted for ordering hundreds of thousands of forced labourers to construct the "Grand Canal" for shipment of goods, thereby linking the south to the north. Emperor Yang was a strong patron of literature and art, and greatly encouraged Buddhist painting and sculpture throughout the nation.

Disastrous military campaigns and internal chaos resulted in the Sui dynasty losing its Mandate to the Tang dynasty (618–907).

The Tang regime was the second long-term centralized and expansionistic dynasty after its predecessor, the Han dynasty. The Tang dynasty had an exceptionally gifted emperor in Li Shimin, the second emperor known as Emperor Taizong (r. 626–649). Many scholars consider him the greatest of all Chinese emperors. He was looked upon as the saviour of society and restorer of peace and unity. His incredible conquests and able administration secured a long and prosperous peace for China. Tang China, while extending her frontiers, took a keen interest in the Silk Road, welcoming foreign export goods, customs and religions. As a result, Tang dynasty culture displays many interesting foreign influences in such things as music, dance, costume and art. Tang China became the most civilized nation in the world and probably the most populous state. China was in constant diplomatic contact with other powers in Western Asia. Other nations were enthusiastically borrowing cultural and political aspects of Tang Chinese society. China won great international prestige and huge numbers of foreigners came to live and work in the Tang capital of Xi'an. It was a "Golden Age" of great cultural splendour for China.

The Tang period was an era of wonderful lyric poetry, strong religious faith, and, in the arts, it was a time of freshness and youth. Art excelled in various forms like painting, Buddhist sculpture, pottery and metal working, and many of these astonishing master-pieces have survived to this day.

In the field of tomb art, the Tang level of excellence has no equal in China. Excavated Tang tombs reveal elaborate construction methods, beautiful murals adorning the walls and lavish art treasures entombed with the deceased. The high aesthetic quality of many of the tomb figurines in Tang era tombs testifies to the remarkable skill of the ceramic craftsmen. Museums in the West are filled with many wonderful examples of Tang grave figures which were never meant to be admired by the living.

In 755 the Tang dynasty suffered a major blow with the An Lushan rebellion. The dynasty did manage to crush the rebellion, but it was never able to recapture its past glory or wealth, and slowly began to deteriorate. Great political and economic confusion arose in the latter part of the dynasty with regional commanders gaining more power. The inevitable destruction of centralized rule was the upshot.

Five Dynasties 907–960 *and Song Dynasty* 960–1279

Following a recurrent pattern, the disintegrating Tang empire broke down in 907 into many dynasties and small kingdoms, all vying for power and independence, and claiming the Mandate of Heaven. The next fifty-three years, called the Five Dynasties and Ten King-doms period, saw the quick succession of a number of would-be imperial dynasties. The southern parts of China remained relatively stable at this time and enjoyed some economic and cultural growth. They copied and maintained a number of Tang cultural traditions. A powerful semi-nomadic, Mongol people called the Khitan who set up the Liao dynasty (907–1125) in north China began making encroachments southward. It is interesting to note that a great deal of their art shows Tang Chinese influence especially in their pottery and Buddhist sculptures.

The Song dynasty was founded in 960 by a powerful Chinese general named Zhao Xuangyin. He was able to accomplish reunification by removing the unrestricted power of regional military commanders. His policy of leniency toward rivals and his extraordinary administrative ability allowed him to set Confucian political standards, which put the dynasty on a firm foundation.

The Song dynasty never achieved the military greatness of its predecessors, the Han and the Tang. They were faced with encroaching powerful foreign dynasties in the north and northwest, the Khitan Liao dynasty and the Tangut Xia or Xi Xia dynasty (1038–1227) respectively. This three way split in the balance of power, however, did provide, at times, periods of peace.

Because Song China was isolated from the West by these hostile barbarian states, she was forced to look inward upon herself and was able to develop a unique culture of great character and high quality. It was a time of ripe maturity and a period of great inventiveness. The learned prose and philosophical speculation of this period was so outstanding that, except for a short period in Greece, there appears to be no equal. Not only did literature, science, philosophy and religion reach new heights of brilliance, the subtle art produced during this period ranks amongst the world's finest achievements. The Song artists carried on the lofty tradition of art passed to them by the Tang and brought it to full fruition, especially in the field of painting and ceramics.

Song dynasty painters are known for their superlative depictions of insects, flowers and bamboos, real and imaginary animals, architecture, portraits of secular and religious figures, but above all, landscapes. Scholars consider the greatest Chinese paintings in existence to come from Song times. This may be due largely to official stimulus, private initiative and historical circumstance. One Song emperor, Huizong, a very talented painter himself, is remembered for setting up art academies to encourage artistic development. Daoism and Chan (Zen) Buddhism at this time also contributed to awakening the artistic minds of the people.

Ceramics made during the Song dynasty reached a zenith. The finer pieces were produced for a social and intellectual elite far more cultivated than in any other period in Chinese history. Extraordinary examples were destined for the maritime trade to other parts of East Asia and the Near East. The brilliant flowering of ceramic art in the Song dynasty reflects the exquisite tastes of the period. The beautiful glazes, decoration, techniques, shapes and styles all display an elegant subtlety and classic purity which are unsurpassed in Chinese ceramics.

Even though the early part of the Song dynasty was more prosperous than any previous dynasty had been, China was faced with huge government deficits caused by population growth, declining tax yield, the cost of maintaining a huge bureaucracy with disruptive factionalism, and the phenomenal increase in military expenditures on the frontiers.

In 1126–1127, the Song capital of Kaifeng was sacked by a new barbarian threat, the Jurched or Nuzhen, who succeeded in capturing two Song emperors. A member of the imperial family escaped to the south, set up his capital at Hangzhou, and tried to re-establish the Song empire in a period known as the Southern Song dynasty (1127–1279). The dynasty would eventually be snuffed out by a mighty Mongol invasion from the north.

Yuan Dynasty 1271–1368

The great Mongol leader, Genghis Khan (*c.* 1162–1227), and his successors established a powerful empire in the 13th century, which included Mongolia, Manchuria, Korea, north and northwest China, Central Asia and south Russia. Their influence also spread across

1.A ***Ding*** ritual food container
Gu ritual wine goblet
Gui ritual food container

2.A   Chisel, *Bi* disc,
Bi disc, *Jue* disc,
dagger-axe

2.B   *Gui* shaped vessel

2.C   Bowl with ring handles

3.A Neolithic vessels

3.B Green lead glazed pottery

3.C Lian container

3.D Greenware ceramics

3.E Changsha ware

3.F Funerary jars

3.G Jun ware ceramics

3.H Yingqing ware ceramics

3.I Yingqing ware

3.J Temmoku ware ceramics

3.K Cizhou ceramics

3.L Ceramic pillows

3.M   Celadon ceramics

3.N   Celadon ceramics

3.O
Monochromes

3.P Monochromes

3.Q   Charger

3.R   Charger
(kraak porselein)

3.5 Pair of large jars with lids

3.T   Yixing ware teapots

4.A Bactrian camels

31

6.A Large four-sided jar

6.B Incense burner

7.A Dragon robe

the Near East to Poland, Prussia, and Hungary. It was not until the rule of his grandson, Kublai Khan, however, that all of China would be subjugated by the Mongols. Kublai Khan became the Great Khan in 1260, set up his winter palace at Beijing, and in 1271 proclaimed the Yuan dynasty. His troops invaded the south and assassinated the last Southern Song emperor in 1279. It became the first time a non-Chinese people would rule all of China.

The Mongols administered their government in China in a military fashion rather than making use of China's sophisticated bureaucracy. The Mongols imposed different laws and customs on the Chinese. The brutality of the Mongols' conquest of China left the scholar bureaucrats suspicious and many went into retirement where they channelled their energy into literature and art. Yuan period drama, in particular, reached a high level. Due to this native hostility, the Mongols employed many foreigners in their civil service. They further antagonized the Chinese by allowing religious tolerance to foreign religions like the Buddhist, Nestorian and Islamic faiths. The Mongols themselves patronized the Tibetan form of Buddhism known as Lamaism. The Mongols reopened the old Silk Road allowing for easy international, diplomatic and religious missions. The world had become more accessible than ever before in the huge Mongol empire.

Kublai Khan was a deep admirer of Chinese culture and built Chinese style palaces with lavish use of gold and brilliantly bold colours. The Mongols, for the most part, were not great patrons of the arts and their taste for bright colours was the very antithesis of the subtlety of the Song dynasty. Painting during the Yuan dynasty went into decline and it was obvious that the master touch of the Song genius had come to an end. Some Chinese artists like Zhao Mengfu did produce wonderful works of art, but the standard of the great age of Song painting could not be maintained.

In the field of ceramics, the Yuan dynasty was a period of innovation and technical experiment, especially at the great kilns at Jingdezhen. It was in the 14th century that the famous Chinese underglaze cobalt blue porcelain underwent its major development. Its shapes and decorative designs were both Chinese and foreign inspired. In the long history of world ceramics, there has been no single ware more appreciated and imitated than Chinese blue-and-white porcelain which was perfected during the Yuan period. As a ceramic tradition, it has the longest continuous development in ceramic history, and has acquired a worldwide reputation unmatched by any other Chinese art form. It may even be the most influential art form the world has ever seen.

By the mid-14th century, the Yuan regime was declining in influence and power, Mongol leadership was disunified, China was suffering from floods and famines, and the country was being overrun by Chinese rebels.

Ming Dynasty   1368 – 1644

In 1368 the peasant rebel leader, Zhu Yuanzhang, founded an imperial dynasty called Ming, meaning "brilliant." It would be the last, great, native Chinese, imperial dynasty. He set up his capital at Nanjing, but his successors would later move it to Beijing. Zhu Yuanzhang was able to reunite the Chinese empire and reconquer lost territories. He revived the civil service examinations and started a system of state schools.

The Ming dynasty was one of the most stable and orderly governments in Chinese history. It quickly established a unified and effective political and social order which would continue largely unchanged until the end of the imperial era in 1911. The dynasty was immensely powerful and sent naval expeditions around the southern seas. It was an important and innovative time for public works, government, law, colonization, literature and the fine arts. The consequence of stability, however, was that things were slow to change in Chinese civilization. Meanwhile in the West, everything was changing and modernization was occurring at a rapid pace.

After the rude interruption of the Mongols, many art forms flourished under the Ming and the dynasty experienced somewhat of a renaissance in the arts. Many artists and craftsmen looked backward to earlier dynasties for inspiration. In some respects, the restoration of old traditions unfortunately left little energy for fresh developments. The Ming period was a great age for scholarship in literature and the arts. Painting was the predominant art form and there were many famous collectors and connoisseurs. Artists were studying and copying the old masters, and painting became a pursuit of men of letters. Ming paintings, while not of Song calibre, showed vitality and innovations, especially in the use of more colour than those from previous dynasties. Professional and literati schools of painting flourished and many wonderful paintings have survived by such great artists as Lu Zhi, Shen Zhou, Tang Yin, Qiu Ying and Dong Qichang.

The porcelains produced at Jingdezhen during the Ming dynasty reached a high level of technical perfection and refinement, especially the magnificent blue-and-white porcelains which would be endlessly imitated around the world. Ceramic masterpieces were produced both for use at home and for export to wealthy patrons in the Near East and Europe.

In the so-called decorative or minor arts, like textiles, lacquer and cloisonné, Ming craftsmen also reached their zenith. They produced magnificent textiles and carpets which were more beautifully woven than ever before. Typical Ming lacquer was red with rich reliefs of floral or pictorial designs, while cloisonné enamelware displayed rich and vibrant colours in a wide variety of bold designs and interesting shapes. During the Ming dynasty, sculpture for Buddhist purposes, both bronze and stone, and monumental sculpture at tombs were in decline. Small carvings in jade, stone, bamboo and wood remained at a highly refined level.

The Ming court, with the exception of the strong rule of the first and third emperors, had rather weak and incapable rulers who were often victims of court intrigue. As time went on and the number of eunuchs at court increased, there was an intensification of corruption at the court. Moreover, Mongols posed a threat on the northern border for much of the Ming period, even kidnapping a Ming emperor, and Japanese pirates menaced the coastline. In the latter part of the 16th century, Ming China began undergoing a gradual decline at home and abroad, and there was mounting peasant discontent. The Ming dynasty fell as a result of an internal peasant rebellion led by Li Zicheng. The Manchu people in the northeast, under the pretext of helping to restore order, invaded China. They promptly installed themselves as emperors in 1644 and set up their own dynasty, the Qing, meaning "pure," which would last until 1911.

Qing Dynasty   1644–1911

The non-Chinese Qing dynasty rulers governed China through Chinese institutions and Manchu military might. The early Qing emperors expanded the empire and after quelling some rebellions were able to maintain domestic peace, which resulted in prosperity and a population explosion. They did try to control the thoughts of their Chinese subjects, especially any sympathy for the previous dynasty. They changed the official dress of the country to reflect Manchu style and forced the men of China to shave their heads and wear pigtails as they did.

The success of Manchu rule over China owed much to two extraordinarily long reigning emperors: Kangxi (r. 1662–1722) and Qianlong (r. 1736–1795), who showed a tolerant and conciliatory policy toward the native Chinese. Both emperors, who are considered among the greatest rulers of China, presided over a prosperous China by a combination of authoritarianism and intelligence through an efficient bureaucracy. Their enthusiastic support for Chinese learning and cultural life as well as their sponsorship of major scholarly projects won them the admiration and approval of most of their Chinese subjects. They were considered classic models of enlightened and cultivated emperors. They centralized power, retained well-disciplined officials and maintained a treasury with a sizable surplus.

Emperor Qianlong ruled China during a golden age when the country was at the height of its dynastic power. Under him, China was the wealthiest, strongest and most populous

8.A (a) Rose quartz and amethyst snuff bottles

8.A (b) Malachite, jade, lapis lazuli, jasper, turquoise snuff bottles

8.A (d)
Glass and
porcelain
snuff bottles

8.A (e) Cloisonné,
mother-of-pearl,
cinnabar lacquer,
lac burgauté,
amber
snuff bottles

◁ 8.A (c) Grey, tan, banded,
macaroni, tan
agate snuff bottles

8.A (f)
Underglaze blue
porcelain
snuff bottles

nation in the world. Emperor Qianlong was extremely extravagant in this time of unparalleled prosperity, and tried to expand the empire farther than ever before.

With great prosperity in the country and cultivated imperial sponsorship, the arts of the Qing period excelled. This was the last great period of Chinese painting in the traditional style. The painting tradition split into several divergent trends between court and literati schools of painting. In the early part of the Qing period, there was a great richness in the range and quality of literati painting styles but a rough distinction may be made between orthodox and individualist styles.

The orthodox literati tradition showed esteem for the great Yuan masters and Dong Qichang. Soft formations of mountains and round patches of vegetation are characteristic of their paintings. The individualists are much less easy to categorize. Some of the greatest of the individualist painters are divided into different groups such as the Eight Masters of Nanjing, the Masters of Xinan, the Eight Eccentrics of Yangzhou, and the monk-painters like Kun Can, Zhu Da and Dao Ji. By the 19th century, Chinese painting was in decline and was little more than a nostalgic evocation of its past glory.

Under the supportive patronage of the Qing emperors, the potters of Jingdezhen attained a mastery of techniques that was never to be surpassed and is often regarded as the culmination of all previous ceramic accomplishments. The potters concentrated their energy and experimentation on the continuous improvement and perfection of the porcelain body and the glazes. Today the porcelain masterpieces of the Qing period are held in such high esteem throughout the world that some experts consider them to be the most splendid ceramics ever crafted by man. The phenomenal amount of porcelain exported around the world during the Qing dynasty earned China great prestige and wealth.

Painting and ceramics were by no means the only art patronized by the Qing emperors. They encouraged workers in jade and precious stones, lacquer, textiles, metalwork, cloisonné, enamelware, and bamboo. A significant number of masterpieces in these media survive.

The decline of the Qing dynasty began even before the death of Qianlong in 1799. Military spending and corruption depleted the national strength; early prosperity resulted in a burdensome population explosion; deforestation and soil erosion caused floods and droughts; and all contributed to making China more susceptible to the superior weaponry of Western imperialism in the 19th century. Pride and ignorance towards the foreigners would compound the calamities. Seven decades of rebellion, especially the formidable Taiping Rebellion from 1851 to 1864, would bring the empire to its knees. The formal abdication of the infant emperor, Puyi, on February 12, 1912 marked the end of the last imperial dynasty and the final loss of the Mandate of Heaven.

Twentieth Century China   1912 – present

On January 1, 1912, Sun Yat-sen came to power declaring the Republic of China. He would resign shortly thereafter in favour of Yuan Shikai, who became president. In 1916 Yuan would even try to re-establish an imperial dynasty and to revive imperial patronage at the kilns in Jingdezhen. The move to become emperor proved so unpopular that he had to resign after only 83 days. He died shortly afterwards and the country fell into a period of warlordism. In 1927, Chiang Kai-shek established the National Government but was soon faced with Japanese invasion. The Nationalists combined with the Communists to resist the Japanese. After the Japanese defeat in World War II, civil war broke out between the Nationalists and Communists, with the latter under Mao Zedong taking power in 1949 and ruling the People's Republic of China to this day.

Some wonderful works of art have been produced in modern China. The most notable would be in the field of painting, calligraphy and woodblock prints. Some of the greatest 20th century artists include Qi Baishi, Xu Beihong, Huang Binhong, Wu Changshuo and countless others who continued to paint in the traditional way.

Bronze Vessels and Weapons

China's Bronze Age culture began in the first half of the second millennium BC and the making of bronze may have been learned from people further west. During the early centuries of this age, bronze was a precious and rare commodity and from the outset, its use appears to have been a jealously guarded monopoly of the ruling class.

Early Chinese bronzes are largely of two types: weapons, which gave the ruling class the physical means of suppressing the remainder of the population, and majestic vessels, which were used in state rituals and ancestor worship by the rulers. The elaborate ceremonial vessels were symbols of power and prestige for the exalted noble ranks and have been treasured in China for centuries. In fact, they are regarded among the ancient world's finest products. These vessels varied in size from small cups and goblets to gigantic cauldrons. The bronzes were often placed in the tombs of royalty and as a result of the chemical reaction with the soil in which they rested for thousands of years, they have corroded and acquired a beautiful patina of various shades of green and blue.

The ceremonial vessels are frequently covered with exquisite decorations executed either in incised lines or in high relief and consist of geometric forms of zoomorphic motifs such as dragons, animals, birds and, occasionally, humans. A prominent and often recurring design is that of the *taotie* or monster mask, which is a frontal view of a flattened animal head centred on the nose with the eyes, horns and ears spreading symmetrically on either side. The angular shapes of many of the vessels with sharp edges and corners shows the aesthetic consciousness and good taste of the Shang (16th – 11th century BC) and Zhou (11th – 3rd century BC) craftsmen. The bronzes were made by various methods, but the majority of the later pieces appear to have been made by the *cire perdue* or lost wax process, which allowed for finer detail.

By the Qin (221 – 207 BC) and Han (206 BC – AD 220) periods, the making of bronze objects continued to be popular, but their role in society had changed from a largely ritual to a more secular function.

Bronze mirrors with intricate designs were made in the Warring States period (475 – 221 BC) and continued to be popular until the Tang dynasty (618 – 907). Because the mirrors could catch and reflect the rays of the sun, they were believed to possess magical powers and were placed in tombs to ward off evil and lighten the eternal darkness of the tomb. On a more mundane note they were frequently presented as wedding gifts.

Jade

Jade has been worked and revered in China for use as sacred objects, for treasure, and for decoration and ornament since Neolithic times. Because of its exquisite beauty, subtle colouring and extreme hardness, jade acquired an exalted position in China at a very early age. The Chinese valued jade more than Westerners did gold and silver. For the rulers of China, it became not only a reflection of beauty, but a symbol of wealth and authority. Because of its rarity, it was largely destined for use by the aristocracy.

Most raw jade destined for China came from the mountains and rivers of Central Asia, thousands of kilometres from the Chinese capital. Since jade is harder than steel, the carving of jade was a long and slow process. The bamboo, bone or metal tools used to carve jade had to be used in conjunction with abrasives such as crushed garnet and quartz sand, which have a greater hardness than jade.

Jade objects have been made in China for approximately seven thousand years and as a result, a great number have survived. Jades in every shape and form served a myriad of functions, but can be broken down into five basic categories: tools and weapons, objects of daily use, ceremonial jades, burial jades, and ornaments.

Jade's durability and special ability to retain a keen edge resulted in its use as weapons and tools in Neolithic China. As time went on, the Chinese endowed jade with mystic power

9.A Dao Ji

9.B Pan Gongshou

9.D Shanghai City

and used it in rituals and ceremonies. The ancient Chinese were totally imbued with the belief that jade could protect a corpse from decay. For this reason, jade objects were placed around the body of the deceased. Various jade plugs and mouthpieces were used as well as full suits of jade encompassing the entire body. Eventually, its functions were more ornamental and it became a popular item to collect. Scholars loved to adorn their desks with jade brush rests, containers, and fondling pieces and women loved to wear jade jewellery.

Pottery and Porcelain

China is famous throughout the world for the important role it played in ceramic development. Its ceramics were held in such high esteem that the English came to call all porcelain "Chinaware." Many Chinese-produced wares inspired later imitations in Europe. For instance, the delicate white *ding* ware of the Song dynasty influenced the potters of Limoges in France and the blue-and-white ware of the Ming dynasty became the prototype of the Dutch Delft ware. The earliest development of ceramic art in China took place in the Neolithic period (*c.* 8000 – 21st century BC) with the production of simple earthenware objects for household and funerary use. By late Neolithic times, magnificent painted pottery vessels in various shapes and with unique designs were being made. It was not until the Han dynasty, however, that ceramic technology started to make a rapid advance. It was during this period that a high-fired and technically well-developed type of pottery was being produced. These pieces varied in quality from roughly modelled earthenware to high-fired stoneware frequently covered by a lead glaze. This technique of lead glazing may have been borrowed from the Greco-Roman world and introduced to China via the Silk Road.

During the succeeding Six Dynasties period (220 – 589), fine quality, porcelaneous stonewares were being made in both North and South China. It is interesting that ceramic vessels of this period often display foreign motifs such as the lotus from the repertoire of Buddhist art, and pearl roundels and lion masks in appliqué from the Sassanian metalworks of Persia.

During the Tang dynasty (618 – 907), Chinese potters began to surpass the rest of the world in technique and artistry. Tang ceramics are noted for the dynamic beauty of their shape and for the development of brightly coloured glazes. Tang potters are most famous, however, for perfecting true porcelain in the 7th century, about eleven centuries before it was achieved in Europe. Porcelain is a hard, translucent ware fused at high temperature with the aid of a high proportion of feldspar causing it to ring when struck.

The Song dynasty (960 – 1279) was the golden age of Chinese ceramics. Song ceramics had a simple elegance that contrasted sharply with the more ornate decorations of the previous dynasty. Much of their output was extremely refined. Shapes were restrained and decoration was reduced to molded or incised relief designs. Colours tended to be soft and sombre – pale blues and green tints, ivory, grey, buff and beige. Among the most famous Song kilns, which produced these superb wares in great quantities in both North and South China, are those of Ding, Ru, Jun, Cizhou, Longquan, Jian and Jingdezhen. The names of the wares usually come from the location of the kiln or their colour.

Following the Mongol conquest of China in the 13th century, a revolutionary change took place in the style and decoration of Chinese porcelain. The greatest ceramic achievement of the Mongol Yuan Period (1271 – 1368) was undoubtedly the development of Jingdezhen where the famed blue-and-white porcelain was produced for the first time. It was destined to become by far the most important of all Chinese ceramics manufactured throughout the succeeding six hundred years and acquired a worldwide reputation unparalleled by any other Chinese art form. It is believed that the technique of underglaze cobalt blue was first introduced to China in the Yuan period from Persia and Mesopotamia where it was already in use on soft earthenware since the 9th and 10th centuries. The Chinese improved the technique to a degree by controlling the blue pigment to allow detailed brushwork in the designs. The Chinese did not have a native source of cobalt free from manganese and therefore had to import it from the Near East. In later years, it came to be called "Mohammedan blue."

From the time the Mongols were overthrown by the Ming dynasty (1368 – 1644) until the 20th century, the history of Chinese ceramic manufacture is virtually the history of the kilns in Jingdezhen, Jiangxi province. Blue-and-white ware produced there became immensely popular and was exported in vast quantities, firstly to southeast Asia, India, and the Near East, and later to Europe.

In addition to the underglaze blue wares, Ming potters at Jingdezhen began to produce a whole range of polychrome objects using a variety of colour combinations such as *sancai* (tri-colours), *wucai* (five colours) and *doucai* (contending colours) wares.

Jingdezhen, though the largest, was by no means the only Chinese ceramic factory during the Ming. A white porcelain with an ivory coloured glaze, which was made at Dehua in Fujian province, was quite magnificent. It came to be known as *blanc de Chine* in the West and was very popular in Europe in the 17th and 18th centuries.

The Qing (Manchu) dynasty (1644 – 1911) continued both the blue-and-white and polychrome traditions of the Ming era. Among the Qing potters' innovations belong the ornate, enamelled polychrome wares such as *famille verte*, *famille noire* and *famille rose* porcelains, which became so popular in Europe in the 18th century. The potters of this period gained complete control of their technique and were continually experimenting with new ideas. They freed themselves from pure ceramic forms and were able to simulate the colour and texture of silver, grained wood, lacquer, bronze, jade, mother-of-pearl, and cloisonné. There seemed almost nothing they could not accomplish and their wares rank among the most splendid ceramics ever crafted by man.

In the 19th century, Chinese ceramics became too ornate or decadent and the craft went into a sharp decline.

Sculpture

Chinese sculpture, for the most part, is related to religion and can be divided into two major categories, funerary and Buddhist sculpture.

Decorating the exterior of tombs with imposing sculptures has been a common practice in both the East and West since ancient times. In China, stone carvings have been placed in front of tombs as far back as the 2nd century BC.

These tomb sculptures marked the beginning of the spirit way (*shen dao*) that led up to the tomb and as a rule was south of the burial mound. It was thought that these carvings not only enhanced the dignity of the tomb and served to glorify the memory of the deceased, but would protect the corpse against evil spirits and prevent any violation of the grave. Numerous ceramic funerary figurines which were found in the interior of the tomb chambers are included in this exhibition.

During the first two millennia BC, both humans and animals were sacrificed at the grave of a man of high rank to accompany the deceased to the next world so as to serve him there as they had done during his lifetime. This practice eventually ended and men and animals of straw, wood or clay (known as *mingqi* or spirit objects) were substituted.

Discovered in 1974, the most famous, clay tomb figurines are the several thousand, life-sized, terra cotta warriors and horses found at the tomb of China's first emperor, Qin Shihuang (died 210 BC).

Ceramic tomb figurines of a small scale became very popular during the Han dynasty (206 BC – AD 220) and continued to be in demand throughout the Sui (581 – 618) and Tang (618 – 907) periods when they reached their highest stage of development. After the fall of the Tang dynasty in 907, the practice of placing clay figurines in tombs began to decline,

9.C

Buddhist
theme of
the Ten
Judgements
of Hell

9.C

but there was a brief revival during the Ming dynasty (1368 – 1644). After that time, the clay figurines were replaced by burning paper effigies at the grave of the deceased.

The style of the tomb figurines changed from period to period and the quality varied from crude, unglazed figurines made from molds to brightly glazed sculptures displaying exquisite workmanship. The size and number of figurines often depended on the deceased's social standing. The wealthier and more important one was, the larger and more numerous were the tomb figurines. The human figurines often depicted court ladies, servants, warriors and entertainers and frequently, horses, camels and domestic animals were represented. Models of carts, houses, furniture and miniature household utensils have also been excavated from the tombs. All these artifacts offer unrivalled material for the study of daily life in ancient China. They reveal the different classes of people once found in China, the costumes they wore, the manner in which the ladies dressed their hair, the armour and weapons of their warriors, their musical instruments, how they danced and amused themselves, the strangers who came from foreign lands to trade with them, how they rode their magnificent horses, the vehicles they used, the architecture of the period, their household utensils, the domestic animals they had, and the animals they hunted. The figurines bring to light the ancient Chinese belief in the supernatural with its demons and mythical animals. All these figurines were placed in the tomb to provide the spirits with necessities and luxury in the next world, and ultimately were an expression of filial piety by the descendants.

The other major category of Chinese sculpture is that of Buddhist images. The religion of the Buddha (the Enlightened One), a North Indian prince-turned-ascetic (563 – 486 BC) spread to Southeast Asia and Central Asia and via trade routes, filtered into China, Korea and Japan. Buddhist missionaries arrived in China as early as the Han dynasty (206 BC – AD 220) to preach the word of the Buddha. Buddhism offered new and stimulating ideas to the Chinese: that existence is suffering, that the individual is repeatedly reborn to lead many lives, and that the soul could escape to an eternal peace. In the centuries of political and social chaos following the collapse of the Han dynasty in AD 220, many Chinese looked to the new religion for salvation. Buddhism made its first great inroads in China during the Six Dynasties period (220 – 589). It eventually spread to the Chinese dynasties in the south. The success of Buddhism in China as well as Asia was partly due to its readiness to adapt to local beliefs.

The expansion of the new religion went hand in hand with that of Buddhist art. The Buddhist images were to be viewed as visual aides (*upaya*) for meditation (dhyana) during prayers rather than objects of worship. The custom of carving Buddhist images in caves began in India, spread to Central Asia and China, and thus, underwent a lengthy evolution of style. Rulers and nobles, in both North and South China, hoped to earn good karma by financing the carving and painting of tens of thousands of Buddhist images in cave shrines throughout China. Some of the most famous grottoes are Dunhuang, Yungang, Longmen, Gongxian, Maijishan, Tianlongshan, Bingling Si and Dazu.

The most spectacular monuments of Buddhist sculpture belong to the Northern Wei, Northern Qi and Tang dynasties. A superb combination of grace and elegance with spiritual expression characterizes the Buddhist sculpture of the Northern Wei. The magnificent upward sweep of form and meticulous detail ranks it among the finest sculpture, whether in relief or in the round, ever produced in China. When Buddhist art first arrived in China, it displayed the stiff, somewhat heavy style of Indian sculpture, but the sculptors in China gradually modified and refined the features, making the details more intimate and human. By the Tang dynasty the images had become life-like in appearance with fuller bodies and rounder forms displaying a flowing, rhythmic style. This was the norm for most later Buddhist sculpture in China.

Most large scale, stone sculpture projects were terminated in 844 – 845 with the great persecution of Buddhism in China , but small gilt, bronze and wooden images continued to be popular.

Applied Arts and Crafts

This section entitled "Applied Arts and Crafts" could just as easily have been called "Miscellaneous." It includes various art forms of valuable, functional and decorative artifacts such as objects made of lacquer, cloisonné, silk fabric, and glass as well as carved bamboo, ivory and rhinoceros horn, to name a few.

Lacquer ware

Another popular craft in early China was the making of lacquer objects. Lacquer is derived from the *Rhus verniciflua* tree which grows over wide areas of China. The natural sap was carefully purified to produce a viscous, clear liquid which could be coloured by the addition of various mineral and vegetable dyes and applied with a brush in thin layers of one hundred or more coats to a certain form, often made of wood. Knowledge of early lacquer manufacture is still incomplete, but its use dates as far back as 6,000 years. By the late Shang period (16th–11th century BC), finely decorated lacquer ware was being produced. During the Warring States period (475–221 BC) through to the Han dynasty (206 BC–AD 220), many lacquer objects like bowls and toilet boxes were made with exquisite painted decorations. Carved lacquer made its first appearance during the Tang dynasty (618–907), but it was not until the Ming (1368–1644) and Qing (1644–1911) periods that exceptionally fine objects showing elaborate cutting technique, sometimes with different coloured layers and a smooth polish, were being produced.

Cloisonné

The technique of cloisonné was probably introduced to China from the West by the end of the Yuan period (1271–1368). Cloisonné is a labour intensive and time-consuming process. Numerous metal wires are affixed in a pattern on a copper or bronze object either by soldering or vegetable glue. Each cell (cloison) is filled with enamel paste and then fired. Since the enamel greatly decreases in volume during the firing, this process is repeated at least four times. After repeated applications and firings, the surface is then ground down so that the wires of the cloisons become visible and level with the enamel. Finally, the exposed metal wires are gilded.

While good examples were being made during the reign of the Ming dynasty Emperor Xuande (r. 1426–1435), cloisonné truly became popular and widespread in China by the time of Emperor Jingtai (r. 1450–1456). During the Qing dynasty, the cloisonné technique was further perfected with the patterns becoming more elaborate and intricate.

Silk Textiles

One of the greatest achievements of China in world culture was the use of silk. China was the first country in the world to raise silkworms for making silk fabrics. Recent archaeological evidence reveals that silk was used to produce garments at least 5,000 years ago. Primitive looms have been found belonging to the Hemudu culture (c.5000–3000 BC) and the Liangzhu culture (c. 3300–2250 BC) in south China and the Yangzhao culture (c. 5000–3000 BC) in the north. By the Shang dynasty (16th–11th century BC), silk was the pre-eminent textile for luxury clothing. The craft reached a high technical level with the making of monochrome silks of plain weave, warp patterned damasks on plain ground, and intricate embroidery to embellish the fabric. During the Zhou dynasty (11th–3rd century BC) and into the Han dynasty (206 BC–AD 220), sericulture and silk weaving underwent rapid development. By the Han period, Chinese silk was being exported as far as Greece and Rome and would become a much sought after commodity for the centuries to come.

The production of silk was a well-guarded state secret and the Chinese were determined to maintain their monopoly on the trade. By the 4th century knowledge of its production spread to other parts of east and central Asia. In the 6th century silkworm eggs

9.C details

Buddhist theme of the Ten Judgements of Hell

were allegedly smuggled out of China to the Byzantium Empire by Nestorian monks who concealed them in a hollowed-out wooden staff. Despite the loss of the secret of silk production, China would remain the chief exporter of silk until the late 19th century.

The magnificent *kesi* or "cut silk" technique was developed by the Tang period (618 – 907), but did not reach its high technical perfection until the Song dynasty (960 – 1279). It is characterized by vertical slits occurring at the line where adjacent areas of different colours meet. Woven on a loom, its designs are made by using the shuttle to open up a space in the background. Hence, the design does not appear as a result of regular changes of the warp and weft, and the front and back are identical, only in reverse. Many fine specimens of this technique have survived from the Song, Yuan, Ming and Qing periods.

Finely embroidered Chinese silk robes used for both ceremonial and practical purposes from the Ming and Qing periods have survived in the thousands. Many can be found in museum collections throughout the world. These costumes are usually richly decorated with embroidered symbols and motifs.

Calligraphy and Painting

The earliest examples of written Chinese characters are found on the "oracle" bones used in divination rites during the Shang dynasty (16th – 11th century BC). As time went on, many styles of writing these characters developed. The same brush and ink are used for calligraphy and painting. Closely related, calligraphy and painting have many points in common. Painting, in fact, probably grew directly out of the use of the brush for writing. To the Chinese, calligraphy is not mere handwriting, but must show originality, style, strength and personality. A fine example of calligraphy mounted as a scroll will receive as much appreciation as a painting.

Painting is an integral part of Chinese civilization and is considered by the Chinese to be their only "true" art. Other art forms, for all their perfection, play a minor role and are regarded as crafts.

Chinese painting takes years of practice to achieve the control of body and discipline of mind needed to master it. It is the only art form that is powerful and lyrical enough to command an equal footing with their poetry and philosophy. As the predominant art form of China, painting conceptualizes much of the beauty and philosophy of life that can be found in one of the world's oldest cultures.

The 5th century art critic, Xie He, laid down the most important set of principles of Chinese painting in his *Critique of Ancient Painting*. His six basic canons he made are as much alive and zealously practised today as they were centuries ago. They are: 1. Creating a life-like tone and atmosphere (rhythmic vitality); 2. Building a structure through brushwork; 3. Depicting the forms of things as they are; 4. Conformity to kind in applying colours; 5. Composition must be consistent, artistic and in accord with the dictates of space; and 6. Live up to the tradition by transcribing and copying the ancient masters.

A 12th-century catalogue, *Xuanhe Hua pu*, classifies Chinese paintings into the following ten groups: 1. Daoist and Buddhist, 2. Human affairs, 3. Palaces and other buildings, 4. Foreign tribes, 5. Dragons and fishes, 6. Landscapes, 7. Animals, 8. Flowers and birds, 9. Ink bamboos, and 10. Vegetables and fruits.

Of all the painting subjects, landscape was the most popular and formed the nucleus of Chinese painting during the last fifteen hundred years. All the skill with which the European artists devoted to portraiture and the depiction of human figures, the Chinese have given to their passionate love of painting Nature.

For the Occidental, Chinese painting is easy to look at, but very difficult to evaluate and appreciate. First, the Westerner must forget his own mental preconceptions, throw out his artistic education, and refrain from making comparisons of Chinese paintings with the famous canvas paintings of Europe. The Chinese are interpreting the material properties of things and living beings in their own distinctive manner. They are attempting to portray an inner poetic reality rather than an outward likeness. They seek to realize rather than to copy nature. Therefore, Chinese works of art should be judged by the inspiration and purpose that lie behind their conception, as well as by the quality of the technique and the nature of the materials at the disposal of the artist.

Chinese artists are impressionists in that they feel free to omit objects which are not essential to their thoughts. Their style never goes to the point of abstraction as there is always a degree of realism present. Their themes and technical approach to painting achieve a unity which is unknown to Western paintings. Their paintings have an underlying simplicity which is in sharp contrast to the photo-likeness of Western painting with its problems of volume, light, shadow and texture. In fact, the Chinese were never interested in the study of scientific perspective which has so engrossed Western artists. When the Chinese wish to give the impression of distance to their field, they resort to their own less realistic but equally valid way of showing perspective. They place the point of view of their composition very high and arrange in groups, one above the other, the objects or persons depicted. The dimensions of the objects and figures become increasingly smaller in proportion as they approach the upper border. In short, what a Western painter would put in the far distance of his picture, the Chinese artist places at the top of his. Another effective method of depicting depth employed in Chinese paintings is the use of graduated ink. Objects in the foreground are painted with dark ink, those further away with lighter shades.

Few Chinese artists work from primary images. Landscapists do not sit with their canvas directly in front of their scene and paint it stroke by stoke. First, they intensely study nature, and then after long contemplation of what they see, they work from memory in the stillness of a studio, attempting to invest the recollection with the profundity of their thoughts.

Peace of mind and mental concentration are so important before the painting begins. Only in this way is it possible for the artist to achieve the perfect co-ordination of mind and hand. With an image of the finished work clearly in the mind's eye, the artist sets brush to paper. A painting can be executed quite rapidly in a matter of minutes with a few splashes and lines here and there (known as *Xieyi* or freestyle). Alternatively, it may be painstakingly built up from numerous, tiny, detailed brushstrokes (known as *Gongbi* or fine style), taking days, weeks or even months to finish. The artist only paints what he considers the essential elements and, in most cases, uses the fewest possible strokes. Preciseness of technique and sureness of hand are vital, for as soon as the artist's vision is committed to paper there is no turning back. The ink line lightly and swiftly laid on paper or silk cannot be altered, erased or painted over. These basic requirements ensure that a Chinese painting is the immediate expression of a man's personality. Chinese painting became, for the most part, the preserve of an aloof and independent class, that of the scholar-gentlemen or literati (*wen ren*). From childhood, they were taught and trained until they achieved a masterly dexterity of the brush. Coming from wealthy families, the literati had the immense advantage of having a long and arduous training which was necessary to master both calligraphy and painting. These literati painters liked to use their paintings as a vehicle to unburden their moments of depression and as a means of expressing their thoughts and emotions. They did not confine their self-expression to painting. Music, poetry and calligraphy were among the other avenues explored.

The four main essentials of the Chinese artist are: a brush, a cake of solidified ink, a stone slab on which the ink is ground and mixed with water, and paper. These are known as *The Four Treasures of the Scholar's Abode*. Each is dependent on the others, and all are highly prized.

Some ten different sizes of brushes are available to the painter. The brushes for delicate work are usually of rabbit hair with the point being so thin that it does not exceed the breadth of a single hair. Those for bolder strokes are of goat or sheep hair. Other types of hair used include the weasel, sable, fox, deer, and pig. Some artists have been known to prefer such exotic materials as wolf hair, mouse whiskers, and even human baby hair.

The brush is held perpendicularly as in the writing of Chinese characters. It is gripped mainly by the thumb, index and middle fingers at a distance of ten to twelve centimetres from the tip. Fingers should scarcely move. For large objects, the arm can be rested on the elbow and on a wrist-rest for fine details. Constant practice makes it possible to set down sure strokes and perfectly modulated lines of continuous strength.

While painting in colours from vegatable and mineral pigments has always been practised in China, the greatest achievements of Chinese painting have been in monochrome. The appreciation of the possibilities of ink in all its shades on paper or silk was the great discovery of the Chinese. The Chinese painter uses a solidified ink cake. The ink is a mixture of lampblack or pine soot and glue pressed into sticks and dried. The artist grinds the cake of ink and mixes it with a few drops of water on a stone slab. Ink may be thick or thin, light or dark (from raven black to a delicate dove grey). An immense range and beauty of tone are possible depending on the amount of water mixed with it. A good artist can produce works of such subtle black and grey shading that a sense of colour can be achieved.

Poetry and painting are also intimately connected. From Yuan and Ming times, it became in vogue for artists among the scholar-painter class, who were also skilled at poetry and calligraphy, to write a poem on their paintings. The poem is often as important to the understanding of the landscape as is the pictorial content. In perfect blending of the three perfections: poetry, calligraphy and painting, it should be difficult to differnetiate which of the three is most important.

Chinese painting has had a prolonged period of evolution. In ancient times, images were painted on ceramics and on walls. As the art developed, silk became the most favoured painting surface. The earliest paintings on silk, so far discovered, are dated between the 5th and 3rd centuries BC. During the Han (206 BC – AD 220), painting came under official sponsorship and paper became a most common painting surface.

The Six Dynasties period (220 – 589) marked the birth of Chinese landscape painting. Landscape painting was further developed under the Tang dynasty (618 – 907) and by the Song dynasty (960 – 1279), it reached its full flowering.

The magnificent development of Song painting owes much to imperial patronage, particularly to the establishment of the Academy of Painting which laid the essential foundation for later academic or court traditions in Chinese painting. Following the takeover of the Mongol Yuan dynasty (1271 – 1368), this type of imperial patronage became less important. With the upper ranks of society failing to promote art, it fell upon scholars and thoughtful people to keep the Chinese painting tradition alive.

After the lean years of the Yuan dynasty, the new rulers of the Ming dynasty (1368 – 1644) tried to restore traditional values and institutions. This meant the reestablishment of the practice of summoning painters to serve at court. These court painters came to be known as the Zhe school. They sought inspiration from the classic landscape painters of the Southern Song period with their misty distances and angular brushstrokes. They were considered professional painters who lived for and by their paintings and who were obliged to produce paintings in accordance with the whims of the court. In contrast to the Zhe school were the scholar-gentlemen painters of the Wu school, who were anti-establishment and created paintings only for their own intellectual amusement. They constructed an ideal art world of their own and carried on the romantic literati tradition of the Yuan masters.

Paintings under the succeeding Manchu Qing dynasty (1644 – 1911) continued along the lines laid down by Ming dynasty painters. The painting tradition, however, split into several divergent trends. In the early part of the Qing period, there is a great richness in the range and quality of painting styles, but a rough distinction may be made between orthodox and individualist styles. For most of the 19th century, Chinese painters tended to look back at what it used to be, and, in many ways, painting became nothing more than a nostalgic evocation of a glorious past.

In the 20th century, classical Chinese painting styles and techniques continued to flourish.

List of Works

BRONZE ART WORKS

COLOUR

BACK COVER

Jue ritual wine vessels
Shang dynasty, Anyang phase,
14th–11th century BC
bronze; ht. 18.6 cm, 21 cm, 19.3 cm
AGGV 88.37.1, 91.7

1.A   (a) *Ding* ritual food container
Western Zhou period, 11th century–770 BC

     (b) *Gu* ritual wine goblet
Shang dynasty, Anyang phase, 14th–11th century BC

     (c) *Gui* ritual food container
Western Zhou period, 11th century–770 BC

BLACK AND WHITE

1.1   *Jue* ritual wine vessel
Shang dynasty, Zhengzhou phase,
16th–14th century BC
bronze; ht. 13.4 cm; AGGV 85.19.2

1.2   *Ge* ritual dagger-axe
Shang dynasty, 16th–11th century BC
bronze; L. 30 cm; AGGV 85.56.2

1.3   *Lei* ritual food container
Eastern Zhou, Spring and Autumn period,
8th century BC
bronze, ht. 26.7 cm; AGGV 92.2.19

1.4   *Yi* ritual ewer
Eastern Zhou period, 7th/6th century BC
bronze; ht. 10 cm; AGGV

1.5   *Dou* ritual food container
Eastern Zhou period, 6th–5th century BC
bronze, ht. 15.4 cm without cover

1.6   Oval vessel with cover
Warring States Period, 5th–3rd century BC
bronze, gilt, copper inlay; ht. 13.1 cm
AGGV 64.237

1.7   *Taotie* mask handle
Warring States period, 475–221 BC
bronze; L. 7 cm; AGGV 92.2.30

1.8   Swords
Warring States period, 475–221 BC
bronze; L. 54.8 cm, 54.2 cm, and 44.5 cm; AGGV 76.87

1.9   Belt-hooks
Warring States period/Western Han period,
4th–2nd century BC
bronze, gilt; L. 7.9 cm, 10.1 cm, and 15.3 cm
AGGV 92.2.13, 92.2.21, 87.33.6

1.10   Ornaments from the Ordos
        Region and other border areas
6th century BC to AD 3rd century
bronze; AGGV

1.11   Mirror
Warring States/Western Han period,
3rd–2nd century BC
bronze, lacquer; d. 14.5 cm; AGGV 92.2.11

1.12   Mirror
Han dynasty (206 BC–AD 220)
bronze; d. 10.4 cm; AGGV 72.129

1.13   Mirror
Tang dynasty (618–907)
bronze; d. 8 cm; AGGV 62.144

1.14   Weights
Yuan dynasty (1271–1368)
bronze; ht. 2.5–3 cm; AGGV 87.33.7-10

1.15   Buddhist temple bell
Ming dynasty, dated 1641
cast iron; ht. 136 cm

1.16   Executioner's sword
Qing dynasty (1644–1911)
bronze, steel, silk cord, leather; L. 90 cm; AGGV 92.40

JADE PIECES

COLOUR

2.A   (a) Chisel
Neolithic or later
late 3rd/early 2nd millennium BC
green jade with white clouding; L. 17 cm; AGGV 92.2.27

     (b) *Bi* disc
Neolithic period, 3rd millennium BC
green jade; AGGV 88.22.5

(c) *Bi* disc

Neolithic/Shang period, 2nd millennium BC
dark green jade; d. 10 cm; AGGV 92.2.28

(d) *Jue* disc

Western Zhou dynasty or later,
11th–7th century BC
grey green jade; d. 10–10.8 cm; AGGV 92.2.33

(e) Dagger-axe

Shang dynasty, 16th/11th, century BC
grey jade with black inclusions; L. 29.5 cm
AGGV 92.2.32

2.B *Gui* shaped vessel

Qing dynasty, 18th century
pale green jade; ht. 5.9 cm; AGGV 77.141

2.C Bowl with ring handles

Qing dynasty, late 18th/early 19th century
mottled dark spinach green jade; ht. 4.7 cm
AGGV 77.146

BLACK AND WHITE

2.1 Beads

Neolithic period, Liangzhu culture
3rd millennium BC
jade; AGGV 92.2.20

2.2 Pendants or inscribers of fish shape

Shang dynasty, 14th–11th century BC
white and pale green jade; L. 11 cm and 5.2 cm

2.3 Pendant of a curved fish

Western Zhou dynasty, 11th century–770 BC
pale green jade; L. 5.9 cm; AGGV 92.2.31

2.4 Ring

Warring States period, 475–221 BC
white jade; d. 6.1 cm; AGGV 92.2.22

2.5 Scabbard slide

Late Warring Sates/Han period, 3rd-2nd century BC
white jade; 10.8 cm; AGGV 92.2.23

2.6 Dog

Tang-Song period, 7th–12th century
greyish white; L. 6.2 cm; AGGV 64.172

2.7 Lion dog

Ming dynasty (1368–1644)
greenish white jade; L. 4.2 cm; AGGV 77.244

2.8 Decorative
bi disc with figure and dragon in clouds

Late Ming/early Qing period, 17th/early 18th century
greenish white jade; d. 20 cm; AGGV 63.111

2.9 Two boys *He be er xian*

Qing dynasty, 18th century
greenish white jade; ht. 7.1 cm; AGGV 68.227

2.10 Jade book with calligraphy
by Liu Yong (1720-1805)

Qing dynasty, Qianlong period (1736-1795)
mottled dark green jade; 11 cm×8.1 cm; AGGV 77.160

2.11 Vase

Qing dynasty, 18th century
white jade; ht. 13 cm; AGGV 77.149

2.12 Vase

Qing dynasty, 18th century
spinach green jade; ht. 11.8 cm; AGGV 77.148

2.13 Belt hook plaque

Qing dynasty, late 18th/early 19th century
white jade; L. 6.5 cm; AGGV 68.225

2.14 Belt hooks

Qing dynasty, late 18th/early 19th century
pale green, yellow, greenish white, white,
white with red artificial stain, jade;
L. 7cm, 8 cm, 8.8 cm, 10 cm, and 9.5 cm
AGGV 75.126, 90.38.12, 90.38.13, 82.62.79, 68.228

CERAMICS

COLOUR

3.A Neolithic Vessels

(a) Large jar

Neolithic period, 3rd millenium BC
Gansu, Yangshao culture, Banshan type
earthenware with black and purplish red pigment
ht. 41 cm; AGGV

(b) Waisted jar with two handles

Neolithic period, 2nd millennium BC
Xindian culture
earthenware with black pigment; ht. 20.8 cm
AGGV 91.14.53

(c) Squat pot with two handles

Neolithic period, 3rd/2nd millennium BC
Ma Chang culture
earthenware with black and ochre-coloured pigment
ht. 12.6 cm; AGGV 91.14.42

(d) Stemmed saucer

Neolithic period, 2nd millennium BC
earthenware with black and reddish brown pigment
ht. 10.7 cm; AGGV 91.14.40

3.B Green lead glazed pottery

(a) Boshanlu censer (lid missing)

Han dynasty (206 BC–AD 220)
glazed earthenware; d. 22 cm; AGGV

(b) Model of Granary

Han dynasty (206 BC–AD 220)
glazed earthenware; ht. 24 cm; AGGV 87.29

(c) Saucer

Han dynasty (206 BC–AD 220)
glazed earthenware; d. 12.5 cm; AGGV 91.14.14

(d) Candle holder in form
of a man holding a child

Han dynasty (206 BC – AD 220)
glazed earthenware; ht. 27 cm; AGGV 88.34.3

3.C *Lian* container

Han dynasty (206 BC – AD 220)
glazed earthenware; d. 19.5 cm.; AGGV 92.1

3.D Greenware ceramics

(a) Chicken head jar

Six dynasties (220 – 589)
glazed stoneware, Yue ware; ht. 16 cm; AGGV 91.46.4

(b) Bowl

Six Dynasties (220 – 589)
glazed stoneware, Yue ware; d. 10 cm; AGGV 91.14.2

(c) Jar with four lugs

Six Dynasties (220 – 589)
glazed stoneware, Yue ware; ht. 13 cm; AGGV 91.46.6

3.E Changsha ware

(a) Pot

Tang dynasty (618 – 907)
glazed stoneware; ht. 14.5 cm; AGGV 91.46.2

(b) Bowl

Tang dynasty (618 – 907)
glazed stoneware; ht. 14.5 cm; AGGV 91.46.2

(c) Plate with incised peony design

Tang dynasty (618 – 907)
glazed stoneware; d. 14.2 cm; AGGV 91.46.1

(d) Ewer

Tang dynasty (618 – 907)
glazed stoneware; ht. 15.2 cm; AGGV 93.14

(e) Leys jar

Tang dynasty (618 – 907)
glazed stoneware; ht. 10.5 cm; AGGV 91.46.3

3.F Funerary Jars

(a) Five spouted funerary jar

Northern Song dynasty, 11th – 12th century
porcelaneous stoneware, Yue ware; ht. 27.5 cm
AGGV 72.77

(b) Five horned funerary jar

Five Dynasties/Song period, 10th – 11th century
glazed stoneware, Fujian type; ht. 25.5 cm; AGGV 72.62

(c) Five spouted funerary jar

Five Dynasties/Song period, 10th – 11th century
glazed stoneware, north Zhejiang type; ht. 27.9 cm

3.G Jun ware ceramics

(a) Deep bowl

Yuan dynasty, 1271 – 1368
whitish Jun ware, stoneware; d. 18.5 cm; AGGV 72.80

(b) Deep bowl

Song/Yuan period, 12th – 13th century
greenish Jun ware; d. 17.5 cm; AGGV 88.22.3

(c) Bowl

Song dynasty, 960 – 1279
green Jun ware, stoneware; d. 10.1 cm; AGGV 91.14.2

(d) Deep bowl

Northern Song/Jin period, 12th – 13th century
dark purplish-blue Jun ware, stoneware; d. 16.8 cm
AGGV 88.37.7

(e) Flat saucer

Song dynasty, 960 – 1279
purplish Jun ware, stoneware; d. 10.7 cm
AGGV 91.14.31

(f) Small bowl

Song/Yuan period, 12th – 13th century
bluish purple Jun ware; d. 8.7 cm; AGGV 88.22.2

3.H Yingqing ware ceramics

(a) Pair of bowls

Song/Yuan period, 12th/13th century
porcelain, Yingqing ware; d.14 cm; AGGV 91.14.2

(b) Statue of old man sitting on a horse

Yuan dynasty (1271 – 1368)
porcelain, Yingqing ware; ht. 12.6 cm; AGGV 91.14.30

(c) Globular jar excavated at
Samar, Philippines

Song dynasty, 11th – 12th century
porcelain, Yingqing ware; ht. 12 cm; AGGV 91.14.1

3.I Yingqing ware

(a) Ewer

Yuan dynasty (1271 – 1368)
porcelain, Yingqing ware; ht.; AGGV 87.36

(b) Small bowl

Song/Yuan period, 13th century
porcelain, Yingqing ware; d. 10.2 cm; AGGV 90.41

(c) Small bowl

Song/Yuan period (13th century)
porcelain, Yingqing ware; d. 11.8 cm; AGGV 91.14.35

3.J Temmoku ware ceramics

(a) Flat bowl

Song dynasty (960 – 1279)
glazed stoneware, leopard spot type; d. 17 cm

(b) Tea bowl

Song dynasty (960 – 1279)
Temmoku stoneware; d. 13.4 cm; AGGV 91.14.6

(c) Tea bowl

Song dynasty (960 – 1279)
Temmoku stoneware, hare's fur glaze; d. 12 cm
AGGV 63.109

(d) Tea bowl

Song dynasty (960 – 1279)
Temmoku stoneware, hare's fur glaze; d. 12.7 cm
AGGV 61.32

(e) Tea bowl

Song dynasty (960 – 1279)
Temmoku stoneware, hare's fur glaze; d. 15 cm
AGGV 67.193

3.K Cizhou ceramics

(a) Covered jar (lid missing)

Jin dynasty, 12th/13th century
stoneware, Cizhou ware; ht. 12 cm; AGGV 88.37.6

(b) Globular jar

Jin/Yuan period, 13th/early 14th century
stoneware, Cizhou ware; ht. 11.3 cm; AGGV88.35.1

(c) Large bowl

Yuan/Ming period, late 13th/14th century
stoneware, Cizhou ware; d. 19.8 cm; AGGV 91.14.28

(d) Deep bowl

Jin dynasty, 12th–13th century
stoneware, Cizhou ware; ht. 9.2 cm; AGGV 88.37.5

(e) Lid

Jin dynasty, 12th–13th century
stoneware, Cizhou ware; d. 12.8 cm; AGGV 81.183

(f) Bowl with calligraphy

Yuan dynasty, 1271–1368
stoneware, Cizhou ware; d. 14.5 cm; AGGV 88.35.2

3.L Ceramic pillows

(a) Bean-shaped pillow

Jin/Yuan period, 13th century
stoneware, Cizhou ware; top 26.4×22.7 cm

(b) Rectangular-shaped pillow

Jin/Yuan period, 13th/early 14th century
stoneware, Cizhou ware; 29.5×15.5 cm

(c) Pillow with curved top

Northern Song dynasty, late 11th/early 12th century
stoneware, Cizhou ware; 15.2×22 cm; AGGV 63.115

3.M Celadon ceramics

(a) Plate

Song dynasty (960–1279)
celadon, Longquan kiln; d. 20.2 cm; AGGV 91.14.29

(b) Conical bowl

Northern Song dynasty (960–1127)
celadon, Yaozhou kiln; d. 15.2 cm; AGGV 91.14.47

3.N Celadon ceramics

(a) Flower pot holder on three legs

Ming dynasty (1368–1644)
celadon; d. 25 cm; AGGV 72.115

(b) Dish

Yuan/Ming period, 14th–15th century
celadon glaze, Longquan ware; d. 31 cm; AGGV 72.108

(c) Bowl

Song/Yuan period, 13th/14th century
celadon; d. 17.3 cm; AGGV 93.3

(d) Drum-shaped jar

Ming dynasty (1368–1644)
celadon; ht. 8.2 cm; AGGV 67.133

(e) Bowl

Song dynasty (960–1279)
celadon, Longquan ware; d. 16.5 cm; AGGV 91.46.4

3.O Monochromes

(a) *Meiping* vase

Qing dynasty, Qianlong (1736–1795)
copper red glazed porcelain; ht. 28.2 cm; AGGV 63.118

(b) Squat globular waterpot

Qing dynasty, Kangxi period (1662–1722)
red glazed porcelain; ht. 9 cm; AGGV 91.14.23

(c) Water pot

Qing dynasty, Kangxi mark (18th cnetury)
peach bloom copper glazed porcelain; d. 13.7 cm
AGGV 64.65

3.P Monochromes

(a) Deep fish bowl

Qing dynasty (18th century)
cobalt blue glazed porcelain; ht. 19 cm; AGGV 72.61

(b) Plate

Qing dynasty, Qianlong mark (1736–1795)
copper red glazed porcelain; d. 21 cm; AGGV 72.110

(c) Plate

Qing dynasty, Yongzheng mark (1723–1735)
imperial royal blue glazed porcelain; d. 16.3 cm
AGGV 91.14.38

(d) Plate

Qing dynasty, Kangxi period (1662–1722)
peacock blue glazed porcelain; d. 20.3 cm
AGGV 91.14.48

3.Q Charger

Ming dynasty, late 16th/early 17th century
porcelain, overglaze enamels, Swatow ware; d. 41 cm
AGGV 93.64

3.R Charger (kraak porselein)

Ming dynasty, early 17th century
underglaze blue porcelain; d. 49.5 cm; AGGV 93.67

3.S Pair of large jars with lids

Qing dynasty, Kangxi period (1662–1722)
underglaze blue porcelain; ht. 57 cm; AGGV 94.10.4

3.T Teapots

Qing dynasty/Republic, late 19th/early 20th century
stoneware, Yixing ware
AGGV 91.54.1, .2, .4, .5, .6, .7, .9, .17 and .39

BLACK AND WHITE

3.1 *Li* tripod vessel (from Xiaodan)

Shang dynasty, 16th–11th century BC
grey earthenware; ht. 9 cm

Ceramic copy of bronze *jue* wine vessel

Shang dynasty, 16th–11th century BC
grey earthenware, ht. 6.7 cm; AGGV

3.2 Pigment container

Shang dynasty, 16th–11th century BC
earthenware with traces of pigment; L. 9.7 cm

3.3 Censer
Han dynasty (206 BC – AD 220)
grey earthenware; d. 20 cm; AGGV 91.14.45

3.4 Pot
Han dynasty (206 BC – AD 220)
glazed earthenware; ht. 15.7 cm; AGGV 84.20

3.5 Bowl with pig-head handle
Han dynasty (206 BC – AD 220);
earthenware, L. 19.3 cm; AGGV 91.46.4

3.6 Bowl
Han dynasty (206 BC – AD 220)
green exterior and yellow interior glazed earthenware
d. 18.8 cm; AGGV 91.14.52

3.7 *Hu* jar
Han dynasty (206 BC – AD 220)
green glazed earthenware; ht. 65.7 cm; AGGV 63.175

3.8 (a) Jar
Six Dynasties (220 – 589)
glazed stoneware; ht. 14.6 cm; AGGV 84.15.2

(b) Stemmed saucer
Six Dynasties (220 – 589)
glazed stoneware; d. 19 cm; AGGV 84.15.1

3.9 Small aquamarine or urinal in the form of animal with open mouth
Six Dynasties (220 – 589)
glazed stoneware, Yue ware; L. 11.8 cm; AGGV 91.14.41

3.10 Vase with loop handles
Sui dynasty (581 – 618)
glazed stoneware; ht. 13.7 cm; AGGV 91.14.4

3.11 Small pot
Sui dynasty (581 – 618)
glazed stoneware, Yue ware; ht 7.5 cm; AGGV 91.14.51

3.12 Jar with lid in shape of lamp tray
Tang dynasty (618 – 907)
glazed earthenware; ht. 19 cm

3.13 Large pot with three legs
Tang dynasty (618 – 907)
glazed stoneware; ht. 16 cm; AGGV 88.37.3

3.14 Jar
Tang dynasty (618 – 907)
cobalt splashed earthenware; ht. 23.3 cm
AGGV 66.19

3.15 Small bowl
Tang dynasty (618 – 907)
glazed earthenware, *sancai*; d. 8.2 cm; AGGV 91.14.15

3.16 Small jar and cover
Tang dynasty (618 – 907)
white earthenware; ht. 11.5 cm; AGGV 91.14.13

3.17 Bowl
Tang dynasty (618 – 907)
glazed stoneware, marbleware; d. 9.7 cm
AGGV 91.14.39

3.18 Jar
Tang/Five Dynasties period, early 10th century
glazed stoneware; ht. 12.5 cm; AGGV 91.14.9

3.19 Circular covered box
Five Dynasties/Song period, 10th century
glazed stonware, Yue ware; d. 8.6 cm; AGGV 91.14.5

3.20 Jar of squat five-lobed shape
Five Dynasties/Song period, 10th century
translucent glaze over white slip, stoneware
ht. 11.5 cm; AGGV 91.14.12

3.21 Ewer
Song dynasty (960 – 1279)
green glazed stoneware; ht. 18 cm; AGGV 91.14.56

3.22 Small bowl
Song dynasty (960 – 1279)
celadon; d. 9 cm; AGGV

3.23 Bowl
Song dynasty (960 – 1279)
celadon, Longquan ware; d. 16.5 cm; AGGV 63.85

3.24 Plate
Song/Yuan period, 13th century
grey celadon; d. 20.3 cm; AGGV 91.14.29

3.25 Large bowl
Song dynasty (960 – 1279)
porcelain, Yingqing ware; d. 20.7 cm; AGGV 91.14.32

3.26 Cup and stand
Song/Yuan period, 12th/14th century
porcelain, Yingqing ware; ht. 11 cm

3.27 Pair of funerary vases
Song dynasty (960 – 1279)
Yingqing glaze; ht. 70 cm; AGGV

3.28 Plate
Northern Song/Jin period, 11th – 12th century
porcelain, Ding ware; d. 18.3 cm; AGGV 94.53.3

3.29 Plate
Northern Song/Jin period, 11th – 12th century
porcelain with copper rim, Ding ware; d. 17.7 cm
AGGV 91.14.27

3.30 Bowl
Jin dynasty (1115 – 1234)
Ding ware type with mould of geese, Jiexiu kiln;
d. 10.8 cm; AGGV 91.14.18

3.31 Jarlet
Yuan dynasty (1271 – 1368)
porcelain with underglaze brown; ht. 6.3 cm
AGGV 91.14.55

3.32 Lady seated on drum
Song/Yuan period, 13th/14th century
stoneware, Cizhou ware; ht. 13.3 cm; AGGV 63.72

3.33 Female figure with basket
perhaps a Daoist Immortal
Yuan/Ming period, 14th/15th century
stoneware, Cizhou ware; ht. 62.5 cm; AGGV

3.34 Owl on rock
Ming dynasty, late 14th/early 15th century
celadon, stoneware; ht. 8.8 cm; AGGV 91.14.16

3.35 Circular covered box
Ming dynasty, 15th century
porcelain, Dehua ware; d. 14 cm; AGGV 91.14.8

3.36 Potiche jar
Ming dynasty, late 16th century
porcelain, *wucai*; ht. 16.5 cm; AGGV 65.67

3.37 Plate
Ming dynasty, Tianqi period (1621–1627)
underglaze blue porcelain with enamels; d. 14.9 cm
AGGV

3.38 Roof tile of rider
Ming dynaty (1368–1644)
glazed earthenware; ht. 28 cm; AGGV

3.39 Two Martavan jars
Ming/Qing period, 17th–19th century
glazed earthenware; hts. 59 and 89 cm; AGGV

3.40 Pair of Plates
Ming dynasty, Xuande/Zhentong period,
early to mid-15th century
underglaze blue porcelain; d. 26.6 cm

3.41 Three-legged incense burner
Ming dynasty, 16th century
underglaze blue porcelain; d. 32 cm; AGGV 72.119

3.42 Bowl
Ming dynasty, late 15th century
underglaze blue porcelain; d. 13 cm; AGGV 82.80.1

3.43 Large bowl
Ming dynasty, late 16th century
underglaze blue porcelain; d. 28 cm; AGGV 91.14.43

3.44 Bowl
Ming/Qing period, 17th century
underglaze blue porcelain; d. 15.9 cm; AGGV

3.45 Mug
Ming/Qing period, 17th century
underglaze blue porcelain; ht. 11 cm; AGGV

3.46 Bowl with quadrilateral mouth
Ming/Qing period, 17th century
underglaze blue porcelain; d. 14.2 cm; AGGV 71.14.6

3.47 Jar with cover
Ming/Qing period, 17th century
underglaze blue porcelain; ht. 39 cm; AGGV

3.48 Bowl
Qing dynasty, Qianlong mark (1736–1795)
underglaze blue porcelain; d. 11 cm; AGGV

3.49 Cupstand
Qing dynasty, Kangxi mark (1662–1722) and
Johanneum inventory mark
underglaze blue porcelain; d. 11.2 cm; AGGV

3.50 Miniature vase
Qing dynasty, Kangxi period (1662–1722)
underglaze blue porcelain; ht. 6.4 cm; AGGV 91.14.20

3.51 Barber's bowl
Qing dynasty, 18th century
underglaze blue porcelain; L. 29.8 cm; AGGV 92.37.1

3.52 Cups
(excavated from the Dutch shipwreck,
Middelburg, 1781, off the Cape of Good Hope)
Qing dynasty, 18th century
underglaze blue porcelain; d. 6.3 cm
AGGV 92.51.1

3.53 "Batavian" bowl and saucers
(Nanking ware excavated in 1985 from the
Dutch shipwreck, *Geldermalsen*, about 1750,
in the South China Sea)
Qing dynasty, 18th century
underglaze blue porcelain with brown exterior
d. of bowl 15 cm; plates 13.7 cm; AGGV 96.8.1, .2, .3

3.54 Candle holder
possibly for Vietnamese market
Qing dynasty, mid-late 19th century
underglaze blue porcelain; ht. 12.9 cm; AGGV

3.55 Statue of Guandi (God of War)
Qing Dynasty, late 18th/early 19th century
porcelain, Dehua ware; ht. 32 cm; AGGV 64.72

3.56 Statue of Budai
Qing dynasty (late 18th/early 19th century)
porcelain, Dehua ware; ht;. 31.3 cm; AGGV 65.66

3.57 Libation cups in shape of rhino horn
Qing dynasty, Qianlong period (1736–1795)
porcelain, Dehua ware; ht. 5.5 cm
AGGV 72.113 and 72.114

3.58 (a) Small *meiping* vase
Qing dynasty, Qianlong period (1736–1795)
porcelain; ht. 11.8 cm; AGGV

(b) Censer
Qing dynasty, Qianlong mark (1736–1795)
porcelain, Dehua ware; d. 12 cm; AGGV

(c) Vase
made for Islamic market
Ming/Qing period, 17th century
porcelain; ht. 20.4 cm; AGGV

3.59 Large vase
Qing dynasty, Qianlong period (1736–1795)
porcelain, guan type glaze; ht. 39.3 cm; AGGV 62.223

3.60 Waterpot in shape of butterfly
Qing dynasty, Qianlong period (1736–1795)
porcelain, robin's egg glaze; L. 8 cm
AGGV 67.135

3.61 Cup holder
Qing dynasty, Qianlong mark (1736–1795)
porcelain, pale blue-green glaze; d. 12 cm
AGGV 91.14.19

3.62 Small vase
Qing dynasty, Kangxi mark (1662–1722)
porcelain, mottled peach bloom glaze; ht. 14.8 cm
AGGV

3.63 Wine cup
Qing dynasty, Kangxi period (1662–1722)
porcelain, *doucai*; ht. 6.4 cm; AGGV 91.14.11

3.64 Fan-shaped sweetmeat dishes
Qing dynasty, Kangxi period (1662–1722)
porcelain, overglaze enamels, famille verte
d. 17.2 cm; AGGV 91.14.49

3.65 Bowl
Qing dynasty, Kangxi period (1662–1722)
porcelain with underglaze blue and
overglaze white and red; d. 15.2 cm; AGGV 91.14.46

3.66 Wine cup
Qing dynasty, Yongzheng mark (1723–1735)
porcelain, overglaze enamels, famille rose; d. 6.7 cm
AGGV 91.14.44

3.67 Water dropper in shape of aubergine fruit
Qing dynasty, Kangxi period (1662-1722)
porcelain, egg and spinach glaze; L. 7.4 cm
AGGV 91.14.10

3.68 Plate
Qing dynasty, Yongzheng period (1723–1735)
porcelain, overglaze enamels; d. 20 cm; AGGV 91.14.36

3.69 Large shallow bowl
Qing dynasty, Kangxi period (1662–1722)
porcelain, rouge de fer enamels; d. 28.7 cm
AGGV 91.14.17

3.70 Eggshell bowl
Qing dynasty, Yongzheng period (1723–1735)
porcelain, ruby red glaze, overglaze enamels; d. 10 cm
AGGV 91.14.21

3.71 Saucer
Qing dynasty, Yongzheng period (1723–1735)
porcelain, famille verte/rose; d. 16 cm; AGGV 91.14.22

3.72 Bowl
Qing dynasty, Yongzheng period (1723–1735)
porcelain, overglaze enamels, famille rose; d. 17.5 cm
AGGV 91.41.24

3.73 Statue of boy
Qing dynasty, Kangxi period (1662–1722)
porcelain, overglaze enamels; ht. 26.2 cm
AGGV 91.41.25

3.74 Bowl with Dayazhai mark
Qing dynasty, circa 1900
porcelain, overglaze enamels; d. 12.6 cm; AGGV

3.75 Pair of semi-eggshell vases
Republic of China, Hongxian mark (1916),
early 20th century
porcelain, overglaze enamels; ht. 14 cm; AGGV 91.41.35

3.76 Vase
early 20th century
porcelain, overglaze enamels; ht. 46 cm; AGGV 94.26

TOMB FIGURINES

COLOUR

4.A Bactrian Camels
Tang dynasty (618–907)
right: glazed earthenware; ht. 65.7 cm
left: earthenware with pigment; ht. 67 cm; AGGV

BLACK AND WHITE

4.1 Standing woman
Western Han dynasty (206 BC – AD 8)
grey earthenware with pigment; ht. 73.2 cm; AGGV

4.2 Farmhouse with pigs
Han dynasty (206 BC – AD 220)
grey earthenware; ht. 30.8 cm; AGGV 88.34.1

4.3 Pigsty with pig
Han dynasty (206 BC – AD 220)
grey earthenware; ht. 12.5 cm; AGGV 88.34.2

4.4 Horse torso and head, and horse head
Han dynasty (206 BC – AD 220)
earthenware with pigment; ht. 42.5 and 9.2 cm; AGGV

4.5 Squatting male with pole
late Eastern Han/Western Jin period, 2nd/3rd century
grey earthenware with pigment; ht. 37.1 cm; AGGV 91.25

4.6 Civil official
Northern Wei dynasty (386-535)
grey earthenware with pigment; ht. 18.2 cm
AGGV 88.37.2

4.7 Female musicians
Northern Wei dynasty (386–535)
grey earthenware with pigment; ht. 11–12 cm
AGGV 88.34.4.1 – .3

4.8 Warrior
Northern Wei dynasty (386–535)
earthenware with pigment; ht. 54.3 cm; AGGV

4.9 Female musicians
Sui/early Tang period, early 7th century
stone with pigment; ht. 20–20.5 cm; AGGV 86.2.1 & .2

4.10 Female attendant
Sui/early Tang period, early 7th century
glazed earthenware; AGGV 93.36

4.11 Male attendant
Sui/early Tang period, early 7th century
glazed earthenware, ht. 2.4 cm; AGGV

4.12 Equestrienne
Tang dynasty (618–907)
glazed earthenware; ht. 41 cm; AGGV 88.36

4.13 Warrior
Tang dynasty, 7th century
glazed earthenware with pigment; ht. 41.9 cm
AGGV 63.112

4.14 Armenian merchant
Tang dynasty (618–907)
glazed earthenware with pigment; ht. 31 cm
AGGV 82.76

4.15 Semitic merchant
Tang dynasty (618–907)
earthenware with pigment; 26 cm; AGGV

4.16 Court official
Tang dynasty (618–907)
glazed earthenware; ht. 45.8 cm; AGGV 88.334.5

4.17 Pair of dwarfs
Tang dynasty (618–907)
earthenware with pigment; ht. 17 cm; AGGV

4.18 Female dancers and musicians
Tang dynasty (618–907)
earthenware with pigment;
seated 19 cm, standing 25 cm; AGGV 87.28.1.1–.6

4.19 Bactrian camel
Tang dynasty (618–907)
earthenware with pigment; ht. 54 cm; AGGV

4.20 Dog
Tang dynasty (618–907)
earthenware with pigment; ht. 13.3 cm; AGGV 88.34.6

4.21 Warrior
Northern Song dynasty (960–1127)
earthenware with pigment; ht. 23 cm; AGGV 88.34.8

4.22 Retinue of officials
Song dynasty (960–1279)
earthenware; ht. 18.7–21.5 cm; AGGV

BUDDHIST SCULPTURES

BLACK AND WHITE

4.23 Buddhist votive sculptures
Tang dynasty (618-907)
gilt bronze; ht. 7.5 and 5 cm; AGGV 92.2.12, 88.17.19

4.24 Buddha bust
Yuan/Ming period , 14th/15th century
wood with pigment; ht. 19 cm; AGGV 61.34.1

4.25 Buddha head
Yuan/Ming period, 14th/15th century
grey schist; ht. 61 cm; AGGV

4.26 Bodhisattvas
Ming/Qing period, 16th–18th century
bronze; large one with gilt pigment;
ht. 25 cm, 51.5 cm, 20 cm, and 23 cm;
AGGV 94.17.15, 68.204, 94.17.4, 94.17.13

4.27 Buddha with attendants
      Kasyapa and Ananda
Ming dynasty, 16th–17th century
bronze; ht. 53 cm and 26.5 cm;
AGGV 94.17.6, 94.17.2, 94.17.7

4.28 Thousand-Li eyes,
      a subordinate to the Empress of Heaven
Ming dynasty, 16th–17th century
bronze; ht. 37 cm; AGGV 94.17.3

4.29 Incense burners
      in the form of Buddhist Lion dogs
Qing dynasty, 19th century
bronze; ht. 25.5 cm; AGGV 72.27.1–.2

4.30 Mythical beast
Qing dynasty, 18th century
bronze; ht. 23.5 cm

LACQUER WARE

BLACK AND WHITE

5.1 Covered box
Ming dynasty (1368-1644)
carved cinnabar lacquer; d. 8.5 cm

5.2 Dish
Qing dynasty, 17th–18th century
red lacquer with guri technique; d. 14.4 cm; AGGV 66.72

CLOISONNÉ

COLOUR

FRONT COVER
One of pair of Buddhist lion dogs
Qing dynasty, circa 1800
cloisonné; ht. 37.5 cm

6.A Large four-sided jar
Ming dynasty; early to mid-17th century
cloisonné; ht. 37.5 cm

6.B Incense burner
Ming/Qing period, 17th century
cloisonné; ht. 36.5 cm without stand

BLACK AND WHITE

6.1 Large dish
Ming dynasty, late 16th century
cloisonné; d. 43.8 cm; AGGV 77.168

6.2 Vase
Ming dynasty, late 16th century
cloisonné; ht. 38.8 cm; AGGV 62.225

6.3 Pilgrim bottle
Ming dynasty, 16th century
cloisonné; ht. 16.5 cm

6.4 Pair of pricket candlesticks
Qing dynasty, 18th century
cloisonné; ht. 54.5 cm; AGGV 77.142

6.5 Pair of flower vases
Qing dynasty, 18th century
cloisonné; 44.5 cm; AGGV 77.169

6.6 Plaque of dragon boat festival
Ming/Qing dynasty, 17th century
cloisonné; ht. 42.2 cm × 48.8 cm; AGGV 77.161

6.7 Waterpipes
Qing dynasty, circa 1900
cloisonné; ht. 27 and 30.5 cm; AGGV 93.5.4, 93.5.4

SILK TEXTILES

COLOUR

7.A Dragon robe
Qing dynasty, 19th century
embroidered imperial yellow silk; AGGV 89.26

BLACK AND WHITE

7.1 Pair of silk tapestry (kesi) panels
Qing dynasty, Kangxi period (1662-1722)
cut silk; 235 × 135 cm; AGGV 77.122
At one time, King George IV tried to purchase these
panels, but was turned down by the owner.

7.2 Elevated shoes and shoe for bound feet
Qing dynasty, late 19th century; AGGV 95.28.1 and 87.31
Wrapped tightly with cloth from the age of five, a
young girl's feet grew painfully into a small
deformed, but erotically admired, shape. The
elevated shoes were worn by Manchu women to
simulate bound feet.

MISCELLANEOUS

COLOUR

8.A Snuff bottles
Qing dynasty, 18th – 19th centuries

- (a) Rose quartz and amethyst
- (b) Malachite, jade, lapis lazuli, jasper, turquoise
- (c) Grey, tan, banded, macaroni, tan agate
- (d) Glass and porcelain
- (e) Cloisonné, mother-of-pearl, cinnabar lacquer, lac burgauté, amber
- (f) Underglaze blue porcelain

AGGV; (See 8.9 for text)

BLACK AND WHITE

8.1 Libation cup
Qing dynasty, 18th century
rhino horn; ht. 13.8 cm; AGGV 92.2.18

8.2 Libation cup
Qing dynasty, 18th century
rhino horn; ht. 7.3 cm; AGGV 67.146

8.3 Libation cup
Qing dynasty, early 18th century
bamboo; ht. 12 cm; AGGV 86.20

8.4 Bowl in the form of lotus leaf
Qing dynasty, early 18th century
bamboo; L. 16.2 cm; AGGV 75.42

8.5 Civil official
Qing dynasty, 18th – 19th century
ivory; ht. 14.5 cm; AGGV 80.16.2

8.6 Belt hook
Qing dynasty, 18th century
hornbill; L. 10.6 cm; AGGV 75.33

8.7 Carved casque of the helmeted hornbill
Qing dynasty, 18th century
hornbill; L. 20.4 cm

8.8 Vase
Qing dynasty, 18th century
glass; ht. 20.6; AGGV 77.171

8.9 Snuff bottles
Qing dynasty, 18th – 19th centuries

- (a) Ivory, cherrywood
- (b) Glass
- (c) Quartz, hair crystal
- (d) Nephrite
- (e) Quartz, crystal; AGGV

Snuff was first brought into China by Europeans as
a type of medicine for nasal congestion during the
late Ming period. It would later become popular with
the imperial court and spread to all walks of life.
Chinese craftsmen changed the foreign snuff
containers into bottles because of China's humid
climate. Chinese snuff bottles were produced in
great quantities during the reigns of Kangxi
(1662 – 1722), Yongzheng (1723 – 1735) and
Qianlong (1736 – 1795). They were fashioned from a
wide variety of materials as can be seen in the
illustrated examples.

CALLIGRAPHY AND PAINTINGS

COLOUR

9.A Dao Ji (1641 – 1714)
Lotus
hanging scroll; ink and colour on paper; 119.2 × 35 cm
AGGV 89.40

This painting is our Gallery's most famous Chinese work of art. Noted art historian, Max Loehr, writes of it. "Done in delicate colour, the close-up vision of the veined leaves in a technically varied, almost mysterious structural design – seems like a poetic anatomy of the plant."

9.B Pan Gongshou (1741–1794)
River and Sky Clearing After Snows
hanging scroll; ink and colour on paper;
70.5 × 29.9 cm; AGGV 88.26.2

9.C Buddhist theme of the Ten Judgements of Hell
(for more details see label information No. 9.19)

9.D Shanghai City
Artist unknown, mid-19th century
watercolour on paper; 49.5 × 111.4 cm; AGGV

BLACK AND WHITE

9.1 Oracle bone
(Inscription – First moon, King's unlucky dream of a son. Translated by Dr. James M. Menzies)
tortoise scapula; L. 7 cm
Shang dynasty, 16th – 11th century BC
The first early form of pictographic Chinese characters to survive can be found in the inscriptions recording divination made on oracle bones of the Shang period around 1300 BC

9.2 Prajnaparamita Sutra, dated 748
Tang dynasty (618–907)
handscroll; ink on paper; AGGV

9.3 Foshuofomingjing Sutra, from Dunhuang, dated 869
Tang dynasty (618–907)
handscroll; ink and colour on paper;
28.5 cm × approx. 500 cm; AGGV 83.65.4

9.4 Sutra with Woodcut Image of Buddha, Laozi and Confucius
Ming dynasty (1368–1644)
printed book; AGGV

9.5 Calligraphy – poem
"The strong current carries a boat as fast as a galloping horse."
"The ancients rejuvenate themselves in spring by feasting on a cooked fish."
Ma Gongyu (1889–1969)
pair of hanging scrolls; ink on paper, 131 × 21 cm; AGGV

9.6 White-robed Guanyin
artist unknown
Southern Song/Yuan period (13th–14th century)
hanging scroll; ink and colours on silk; 87.8 × 39 cm
AGGV

9.7 Lu Zhi (1496–1575)
Magnolias
hanging scroll; ink and colours on paper; 143.5 × 57.1
AGGV 77.120

9.8 Lan Ying (1585 – c. 1664)
Landscape fan painting; ink and colours on gold paper
16.7 × 55.6 cm; AGGV 68.13

9.9 Huang Daozhou (1585–1646)
Landscape
fan painting; ink on gold paper; 16 × 50.4 cm; AGGV 65.1

9.10 Gong Xian (1617/18–1689)
Landscape
album leaf as hanging scroll; ink on paper;
22.9 × 52.1 cm; AGGV 65.2

9.11 Li Shan (c. 1675/85 – 1755/62)
Lily
album leaf as hanging scroll; ink on paper
25.3 × 38 cm; AGGV 85.5

9.12 Hua Yan (1682–1765)
Butterfly and Iris
album leaf; ink and colour on paper; 32 × 37 cm
AGGV 93.71.2

9.13 Hua Yan (1682–1765)
Cricket and spider on grass
album leaf; ink and colour on paper; 32 × 37 cm
AGGV 93.71.1

9.14 Zou Zhe (1636–1708)
Landscape
hanging scroll; ink and colours on paper; 100.2 × 4 cm
AGGV 83.20

9.15 Ma Quan (a woman painter active late 17th/early 18th century)
Autumn Flowers, 1714
hanging scroll; ink and colours on silk; 90 × 41 cm
AGGV 64.71

9.16 Gu Jianlong (1606 – c. 1687) Attributed
Metamorphosis of the Heavenly Spirits (detail)
handscroll; ink and colours on silk; 33 × 400 cm
AGGV 68.156

9.17 Yuan Jiang (active c. 1690–1724) Attributed
Wonderful View of Penglai in Autumn
hanging scroll; ink and colours on silk
152.5 × 159 cm; AGGV 64.38

9.18 Portrait of Mr. Wang Shilun (?), descendant of Song Imperial House
Artist unknown
Ming/Qing period, 17th/18th century
scroll; ink and colours on paper; 167 × 95.5 cm

9.19 Buddhist Theme of the Ten Judgments of Hell
details, nine of set of ten
Unknown court painter
late Ming/early Qing period, 17th century
hanging scrolls; ink and colour on paper; 156 × 88 cm
AGGV 89.46

The subject matter of the set of scrolls is the Buddhist theme of the Ten Judgments of Hell. Each scroll depicts a different set of vices with associated punishments as determined by the [Pure Land] Buddhist faith. Such scrolls were originally used in temples to illustrate concepts of punishment and the over-whelming images surely instilled fear of deviating from morality in many individuals. The concept of punishment to the soul as a consequence of actions in life through an endless cycle of rebirth was a central tenet to the Pure Land Buddhist sect. Although at one time such sets of scrolls were quite common, they are now exceedingly rare due to the passage of time and, particularly, destruction during the period of the Communist take-over of China. Hell scrolls were disdained by Chinese scholars and were rarely preserved after their use. They now have become valuable historic records of the folk art and religion of China. This set is undoubtedly among the oldest surviving sets. To date, we have only been able to determine one complete set of this age and that is in the collection of the Berlin Museum. The Metropolitan Museum of Fine Art in New York, the Fogg Art Museum at the Harvard University and the Asian Art Museum of San Francisco also have some scrolls from a set.

The ten hells, or underground prisons, are each governed by a King or Judge and each specializes in the punishment of specific sins. They are usually portrayed as honourable Chinese bureaucratic judges. The entire establishment is under the rule of the bodhisattva, Di Zang. The King of the first hell, Qin Guang, whose status is higher than that of the other nine kings, performs the initial evaluation of the dead souls. Those whose good deeds outweigh their transgressions, are reborn into the world without undergoing punishment and the rest are punished in accordance with their particular misdeeds. The types of misconduct range through such crimes as dishonest marriage brokerage, officials who have accepted bribes, people who have kidnapped boys to sell to monks, grave robbers, practice of cannibalism, etc. The torture punishments on the pathetic human beings or souls are performed by various monsters and demons. Gory and far-fetched punishments take place in hell such as dogs gnawing on limbs, bodies being sawed in half, disembowelment, grinding bodies in a wheat-grinding mill, impaling bodies on spikes, boiling people in cauldrons and so on.

Some souls are condemned to remain in hells forever, but some souls of those who have completed their course of punishment are sent to the tenth hell where they wait to be reborn. The king of this hell assigns the souls to their next place of birth in the world, determining whether it will be in human or animal form and what rank and degree of happiness it will enjoy, all on the basis of past actions. Each soul is made to drink broth that wipes out the memory of what it has undergone, after which it is thrown into a river of crimson water that carries it to its new birth.

9.20 Judgment of Hell
one of set of ten

Artist unknown
Qing dynasty, circa 1800
hanging scroll; ink and colour on paper; 156×88 cm
AGGV 89.46

9.21 Ren Yi (1840–1896)
Boy with buffalo
hanging scroll; ink and colours on paper
88×32.8 cm; AGGV

9.22 Empress Ci Xi (1835–1908) Attributed
With calligraphy by Jun Xiang (1841–1915)
Rocks and Epidendra
hanging scroll; ink on paper; 198.5×81.4 cm
AGGV 69.113

9.23 Qi Baishi (1863–1957)
Chrysanthemums
hanging scroll; ink and colours on paper; 160×37 cm
AGGV

9.24 Xu Beihong (1896–1953)
Prunus
hanging scroll; ink and colours on paper;
81.3×14.3 cm; AGGV

9.25 Shi Lu (1919–1982)
Pine Tree
hanging scroll; ink and colours on paper;
67.8×52.7 cm; AGGV

1.1 *Ding* ritual food container

1.2 *Ge* ritual dagger-axe

1.3 *Lei* ritual food container

1.4 *Yi* ritual ewer

63

1.5 **Dou** ritual food container

1.6 Oval vessel with cover

1.7 **Taotie** mask handle

1.9 Belt-hooks

1.8 Swords

1.11 Mirror

1.10 Ornaments from the Ordos region and other border areas

1.12 Mirror

1.14 Weights

1.13 Mirror

66

1.15 Buddhist temple bell

1.16 Executioner's sword

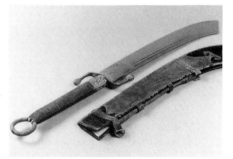

1.16 (Detail) translation – Destroy the violent, to bring peace to the community.

2.1   Beads

2.2
Pendants or
inscribers
of fish shape

2.2

2.3   Pendant of a curved fish

2.4   Ring

68

2.5 Scabbard slide

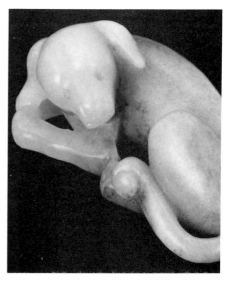

2.7 Lion dog

2.6 Dog

2.8 Decorative *bi* disc

2.9 Two boys *He be er xian*

2.10 Jade book with calligraphy

2.11 Vase

2.12 Vase

2.13 Belt hook plaque

2.14 Belt hooks

71

3.1 *Li* tripod vessel

3.1 Ceramic copy of bronze *jue* wine vessel

3.2 Pigment container

3.3 Censer

72

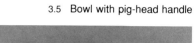

3.4 Pot

3.6 Bowl

3.7 *Hu* jar

3.9 Small aquamarine or urinal

3.8 *left* Jar
right Stemmed saucer

3.11 Small pot

3.10 Vase with loop handles

3.12 Jar with lid

3.13 Large pot with three legs
(detail)

3.14 Jar

3.15 Small bowl

3.16 Small jar and cover

3.17 Bowl

3.18 Jar

3.19 Circular covered box
(detail)

3.21 Ewer (detail)

3.20 Jar (detail)

3.23 Bowl

3.24 Plate

3.22 Small bowl

3.25 Large bowl

3.27 Pair of funerary vases   3.28 Plate (detail)

3.26 Cup and
      stand

79

3.29 Plate (detail)

3.31 Jarlet

3.30 Bowl (detail)

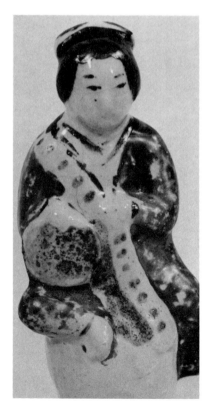

3.32 Lady seated on drum

3.33 Female figure with basket

3.34 Owl on rock

3.35 Circular covered box

3.36 Potiche jar

◁ 3.38 Roof tile of rider

3.37 Plate (detail)

3.39 Two Matelban jars (detail)

3.40 Pair of plates

3.41 Three-legged incense burner

3.42 Bowl

3.43 Large bowl

3.45 Mug

3.46 Bowl with quadrilateral mouth

3.47 Jar with cover

3.48 Bowl (detail)

3.49 Cupstand (detail)

3.50 Miniature vase

3.51 Barber's bowl

3.52 Cups

3.53
"Batavian"
bowl and saucers

3.55 Statue of Guandi

3.54 Candle holder

3.56 Statue of Budai

3.57
Pair of libation cups (detail)

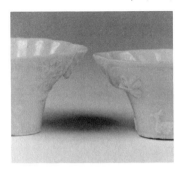

3.60 Waterpot

3.58 *left* Small *meiping* vase   *centre* Censer   *right* Vase

3.59 Large vase

3.61 Cup holder

3.63 Wine cup (detail)

3.64 Fan-shaped sweetmeat dishes

3.65 Bowl

3.66 Wine cup

3.67 Water dropper

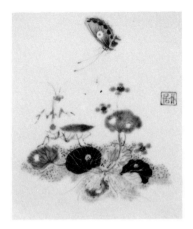

3.68 Plate (detail)

3.69 Plate
(detail)

3.70 Eggshell bowl (detail)

3.73 Statue of boy

91

3.72 Bowl

3.71 Saucer

3.74 Bowl with Dayazhai mark (detail)

3.76 Vase

3.75 Pair of semi-eggshell vases

4.1 Standing woman

4.2 Farmhouse with pigs

4.4
Horse torso and head,
and horse head

4.3 Pigsty with pig

4.5 Squatting male with pole

4.6 Civil official

4.7 Female musicians

95

4.8 Warrior

4.9 Female musicians

4.10 Female attendant

4.11 Male attendant

4.12 Equestrienne

4.13 Warrior

4.14
Armenian
merchant

97

4.15
Semitic
merchant

4.16
Court
official

4.17   Pair of dwarfs

4.18   Female dancers and musicians

4.18 detail

4.20 Dog

4.19 Bactrian camel

4.22 Retinue of officials

4.21 Warrior

4.23 Buddhist votive sculptures

4.25 Buddha head

4.24
Buddha
bust

4.26
Bodhisattvas

4.27 Buddha with attendants

4.28 Thousand-Li eyes

4.29 Incense burners

4.30 Mythical beast

5.2 Dish

5.1 Covered box

103

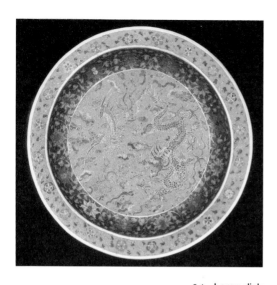

6.1 Large dish

6.3 Pilgrim bottle

6.2 Vase

6.4
Pair of pricket
candlesticks

6.6 Plaque of
dragon boat festival
(detail)

6.5 Pair of flower vases

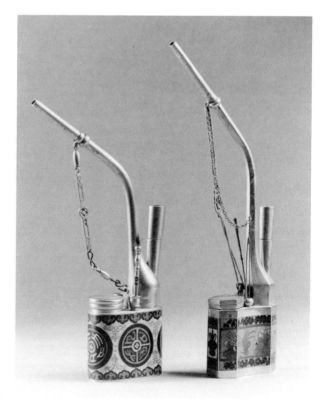

6.7 Waterpipes

105

7.1 Pair of silk tapestry (kesi) panels

7.2 Elevated shoes and shoe for bound feet

8.2 Libation cup (detail)

8.1 Libation cup

8.3 Libation cup

8.4 Bowl in the form of lotus leaf (detail)

8.5 Civil official

8.8 Vase

8.6 Belt hook

8.7 Carved casque
of the helmeted hornbill

8.9 (a) Ivory, cherrywood snuff bottles

8.9 (b) Glass snuff bottles

8.9 (c) Quartz, hair crystal snuff bottles

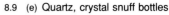

8.9 (d) Crystal and nephrite snuff bottles

9.1 Oracle bone

9.2 Prajnaparamita Sutra

般若波羅蜜多經

大唐天寶七載四月八日佛弟子索瓀
為妣
此微福顧尊靈遊越三途栖神淨土及
去男冥主一乘成佛

婆等聞佛所說皆大歡喜信受奉行

塞優婆夷并諸菩薩一切世間天人阿修羅乾闥
佛說是經已尊者湏菩提及諸比丘比丘尼優婆

如是開示是故說名真實開示
於一切有為
如星翳燈幻
露泡夢電雲
應作如是觀

說真實開示由此因緣所生福聚甚多於彼無量
無數云何真實開示如然而開示

奉施諸佛如來復有善男子或善女人於此般若
波羅蜜多法門乃至四句偈等受持讀誦為人演

110

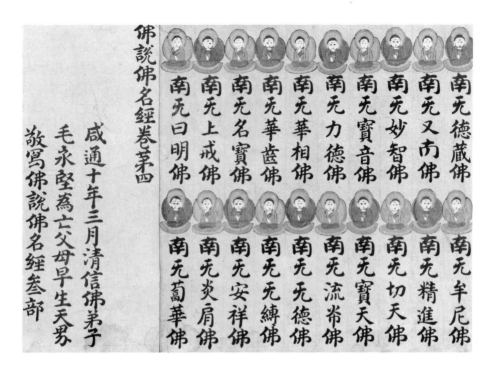

佛說佛名經卷第四

南无德藏佛
南无牟尼佛
南无又市佛
南无精進佛
南无妙智佛
南无切天佛
南无寶音佛
南无寶天佛
南无力德佛
南无流帝佛
南无華相佛
南无无德佛
南无華遊佛
南无无縛佛
南无名寶佛
南无安祥佛
南无上戒佛
南无炎肩佛
南无日明佛
南无蒚華佛

咸通十年三月清信佛弟子
毛永堅爲亡父母早生天界
敬寫佛說佛名經叁部

9.3 Foshuofomingjing Sutra

皇圖永固 帝道遐昌
佛日增輝 法輪常轉

9.4 Sutra with woodcut image of Buddha

111

9.6
White-robed Guanyin

9.5 Calligraphy—poem

9.7
Lu Zhi

112

9.8 Lan Ying, fan (detail)

9.9 Huang Daozhou

113

9.10 Gong Xian

9.11 Li Shan

9.12 Hua Yan (detail)

114

9.13 Hua Yan

9.14 Zou Zhe

9.15 Ma Quan

9.16 Gu Jian Long (detail)

115

9.17 Yuan Jiang

9.18 Portrait of Mr. Wang Shilun (?)

9.19 (a) Buddhist Theme of the
Ten Judgments of Hell (detail)

9.19 (b) detail

9.19 (c) detail

9.19 (d) detail

9.19 (e) detail

9.19 (f) detail

9.20 Judgment of Hell

9.22 Empress Ci Xi

9.21 Ren Yi

119

9.23 Qi Baishi

9.24 Xu Beihong

9.25 Shi Lu

List of Works / Donor Information

1. Miss Kathleen Agnew Purchase Fund: 1.13
2. Gift of the American Friends of Canada Committee, Inc. through the generosity of Mr. Robert H. Falk: 4.A(a)
3. Gift of Mrs. Sheila Anderson: 3.D(a) & (c), 3.E(a) (b) (c)& (e), 3.N(e), 3.5
4. Anonymous Gifts: 3.K(e), 3.23, 4.A(b), 4.26, 4.27, 4.28, 9.9
5. In Memory of Edward W. Beltz (1891-1970): 4.10
6. Gift of John Boehme: 3.I(b)
7. Gift of Anita Boyd: 2.A(b), 3.G(b) & (f)
8. Gift of Mary Boyle Estate: 3.76
9. Given by Professor James Caswell in honour of his parents, Mae E. and Oliver Caswell: 9.6
10. Gift from J. M. Plumer to the donor Mrs. J. A. Chapman: 3.J(c)
11. Gift of the Chen King Foh family: 1.12, 3.F(a) & (b), 3.G(a), 3.N(a) & (b), 3.P(a) & (b), 3.41, 3.46, 3.57, 4.29
12. Gift of Renée Chipman: 7.1
13. Gift of Ramsey Gordon Cooper: 3.R
14. Gift of Cheney Cowles: 3.C
15. Gift of Ernie A. Davis: 9.C, 9.19, 9.20
16. Gift of Mr. & Mrs. R. W. Finlayson: 1.2, 4.18, 4.25, 9.A, 9.B, 9.7, 9.12, 9.13
17. Gift of Dr. and Mrs. Arnold Frenzel: 9.D
18. Gift of Captain L. J. M. Gauvreau: 6.2
19. Mrs. Massy Goolden Fund: 2.8, 3.L(c), 3.0(a), 3.7, 4.13
20. Gift of Mrs. Percy Gotz: 8.5
21. Gift of Mrs. Kathleen Graham: 3.59
22. Gift of Jack Guthrie: 3.53
23. Gift of Syd Hoare: 3.14, 3.36, 3.37, 3.38, 3.44, 3.45, 3.48, 3.49, 3.54, 3.55, 3.56, 3.58, 3.62, 3.74, 9.15
24. Gift of Mary Hummel: 1.16
25. Gift of S. W. Jackman: 3.S
26. Gift of Dr. Ben Kanee: 4.14
27. J. P. E. Klaverwyden Bequest: 3.J(e), 3.N(d), 4.26(b), 9.16, 9.22
28. Gift of Edith Low-Beer Estate: 2.14(b) & (c)
29. Gift of Lund's Auction Purchase Fund: 7.2(a)
30. Gift of Kathleen Wilson Lambert Marpole: 3.22
31. Gift of Brian S. McElney: 1.1, 1.3, 1.7, 1.9(b) & (c), 1.10(e) & (f), 1.11, 2.A (a) (c) (d)&(e), 2.1, 2.3, 2.4, 2.5, 3.A, 3.B(c) & (d), 3.D(b), 3.G(c) & (e), 3.H, 3.I(c), 3.J(b), 3.K(c), 3.M, 3.0(b), 3.P(c) & (d), 3.3, 3.6, 3.9, 3.10, 3.11, 3.15, 3.16, 3.17, 3.18, 3.19, 3.20, 3.21, 3.24, 3.25, 3.29, 3.30, 3.31, 3.34, 3.35, 3.42, 3.43, 3.50, 3.61, 3.63, 3.64, 3.65, 3.66, 3.67, 3.68, 3.69, 3.71, 3.72, 3.73, 3.75, 4.1, 4.2, 4.3, 4.7, 4.9, 4.16, 4.20, 4.21, 4.23(a), 8.1, 8.3, 8.4, 9.11, 9.21, 9.23, 9.24, 9.25
32. Rev. James M. Menzies Family Collection:

    Gift of Arthur R. Menzies in memory of his father, Rev. Dr. James M. Menzies: 9.2, 9.3, 9.4, Loan: Back cover (a), 1.5, 1.8, 2.2, 3.2, 3.J(a), 3.26, 5.I

    Gift of Frances Menzies Newcombe: Back cover (b), 3.G(d), 3.K(a) & (d), 3.13, 4.6, 4.23(b), Loan: 1.8(c), 3.L(a), 3.40, 9.1

    Gift of Marion Menzies Hummel and James Menzies Hummel: Back cover (c), 3.1(b), 3.K(b) & (f), 3.28, 4.11, 4.12, Loan: 3.1(a), 3.F(c), 3.L(a), 3.40
33. Gift of Robert Fenwick Miller: 3.Q
34. Gift of Mary Morrison: 3.4, 3.8
35. Harold and Vera Mortimer-Lamb Bequest: 2.7
36. Harold and Vera Mortimer-Lamb Purchase Fund: 3.52, 4.5
37. Gift of Carol Potter Peckham: 3.T
38. Fred and Isabel Pollard Collection: 2.6, 2.9, 2.13, 2.14, 3.0(c), 3.32, 3.60, 5, 5.2, 8.2, 9.8, 9.10, 9.17
39. Private Collections: Front cover, stone relief at end, 1.A, 4.30, 8.7, 9.18
40. The Reid Collection: 6.A, 6.B, 6.3
41. Gift of Mrs. M. H. Roffey: 8.6
42. Gift of Mrs. R. I. Ross: 7.A
43. Gift of Helen Sawyer: 8.A, 8.9
44. Gift of Mina Sherman: 7.2(b)
45. Gift of Mr. Etienne Sigaut: 1.6, 1.8(b)
46. Gift of Nancy Simpson: 9.D
47. Gift of Anne M. Storey: 6.7
48. Given anonymously in Memory of Sir James Howard Thornton, CB, MB, BA: 2.B, 2.C, 2.10, 2.11, 2.12, 6.1, 6.4, 6.5, 6.6, 8.8
49. City of Victoria: 1.15
50. Gift of Basil Wallace: 3.N(c), 4.14, 9.13
51. Gift of Gerald Weisbrod: 1.9(a), 1.14, 3.I(a)
52. Gift of Mrs. P. S. Widdup: 2.14(d)
53. Gift of Mr. A. S. Wylie: 4.24
54. Women's Committee Cultural Fund Purchase: 3.J(d)
55. Gift of Mr. Irving Zucker: 1.4, 3.B(a), 3.27, 3.33, 3.39, 3.47, 4.4, 4.8, 4.15, 4.17, 4.22

Cahill, James, *Chinese Painting*, Lausanne, 1960.

Cheng Te-k'un, *Archaeology in China*, Vols. I and II, Cambridge, 1960, 1963.

Fitzgerald, C. P., *China: A Short Cultural History*, New York, 1961.

Fong, Wen, *The Great Bronze Age of China*, London, 1980.

Fontein, Jan and Wu, Tung, *Unearthing China's Past*, Boston, 1973.

Forsyth, Angus and McElney, Brian S., *Jades from China*, 1994.

Hansford, S. Howard, *Chinese Carved Jades*, Greenwich, 1968.

Ho, Wai-Kam et al., *Eight Dynasties of Chinese Painting*, Cleveland, 1980.

Idemitsu Museum of Art, *In Pursuit of the Dragon*, Seattle, 1988.

Jenyns, R. Soame and Watson, William, *Chinese Art II and III*, New York, 1966.

Kuwayama, George, et al., *The Quest for Eternity*, Los Angeles and San Francisco, 1987.

La Plante, John D., *Arts of the Chou Dynasty*, Stanford, 1958.

Lion-Goldschmidt, Daisy and Moreau-Gobard, Jean-Claude, *Chinese Art*, New York, 1966.

Loehr, Max, *The Great Painters of China*, Oxford, 1980.

McElney, Brian S., *The Museum of East Asian Art, Bath, England Inaugural Exhibition, Vols. I & II*, Bath, 1993.

Rawson, Jessica, *Ancient China, Art and Archaeology*, London, 1980.

———, *Chinese Bronzes, Art and Ritual*, London, 1987.

Rawson, Jessica (ed.), *The British Museum Book of Chinese Art*, London, 1992

Royal Ontario Museum, *Homage to Heaven, Homage to Earth*, Toronto, 1992.

Schloss, Ezekiel, *Ancient Chinese Ceramic Sculpture: From Han Through T'ang*, Stamford, 1977.

Sickman, Laurence and Soper, Alexander, *The Art and Architecture of China*, Harmondsworth, 1956.

Sullivan, Michael, *The Arts of China*, Berkeley, Los Angeles, London, 1977.

Tregear, Mary, *Chinese Art*, London, 1980.

Thorp, Robert L., *Son of Heaven, Imperial Arts of China*, Seattle, 1988.

Watson, William, *Style in the Arts of China*, New York, 1980.

Willetts, William, *Foundations of Chinese Art*, New York, London and Toronto.

Chronology

Neolithic	*c.* 8000 – 21st century BC
Xia	21st – 16th century BC
Erlitou Culture	19th – 16th century BC
Shang	16th – 11th century BC
Zhou	11th – 3rd century BC
Western Zhou	11th century – 771 BC
Eastern Zhou	770 – 221 BC
Spring and Autumn period	770 – 476 BC
Warring States period	475 – 221 BC
Qin	221 – 207 BC
Han	206 BC – AD 220
Western Han	206 BC – AD 8
Xin (Wang Mang)	AD 8 – 23
Eastern Han	AD 23 – 220
Six Dynasties	AD 220 – 589
Sui	AD 581 – 618
Tang	AD 618 – 907
Five Dynasties	AD 907 – 960
Song	AD 960 – 1279
Northern Song	AD 960 – 1127
Southern Song	AD 1127 – 1279
Liao Dynasty (Khitan)	AD 907 – 1125
Jin Dynasty (Jurchen)	AD 1115 – 1234
Yuan	AD 1271 – 1368
Ming	AD 1368 – 1644
Qing	AD 1644 – 1911
Republic of China	1912 – 1949
People's Republic of China	1949 –

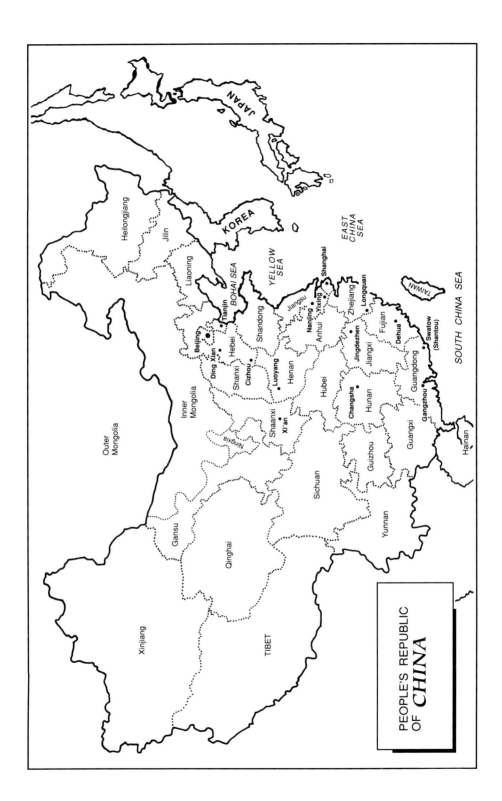

PEOPLE'S REPUBLIC OF CHINA

Far Eastern Publications
of the Art Gallery of Greater Victoria

Early Korean Ceramics from the Syd Hoare Collection, by Colin Graham, 1966.

Kamakura to Edo, by Colin Graham, 1967.

Japanese Art at the Art Gallery of Greater Victoria, by John Vollmer and Glenn T. Webb, 1972.

Mokuhan: The Woodcuts of Munakata and Matsubara, by Joan Stanley-Baker, 1977.

The Inner Eye of Chen Chi-Kuan, by Joan Stanley-Baker, 1977.

The Arts of Tibet: Painting, by Doug Henderson, 1977.

Ukiyo-e: Glimpses into the Floating World, by Patricia Wright, 1977.

The Calligraphy of Kan Makiko, by Joan Stanley-Baker, 1978.

Chinese Ceramic Handbook, by Mary Tregear, 1978.

Mingei: Folkcrafts of Japan, by Joan Stanley-Baker, 1979.

Japanese Lacquer, by Joan Stanley-Baker and Robert Amos, 1980.

Nanga: Idealist Painting of Japan, by Joan Stanley-Baker, 1980.

An Introduction to Japanese Art, by Robert Amos, 1980.

Ceramics of the Yuan Dynasty and Their Influence, by Claire Gunn, 1980.

Japanese Sen Cha Ceremony Utensils, by Colin Graham, 1981.

The Art of China's Bronze Age, by James O. Caswell, 1982.

Ceramics: East Meets West, by Patricia Bovey and Barry Till, 1982.

Chinese Paintings in Canadian Collections, by Barry Till, 1982.

Antique Cinese Cloisonné, by Barry Till and Paula Swart, 1983.

Porcelain of the High Qing Period (1662-1795), by Barry Till, 1983

The Flowering of Japanese Ceramic Art, by Barry Till and Paula Swart, 1983.

Japanese Paintings in Canadian Collections, by Barry Till, 1983.

Japanese Modern Prints, by Barry Till, 1984.

Samurai, the Cultured Warrior, by Barry Till, 1985.

A Selection of Twentieth Century Chinese Paintings, by Barry Till, 1985.

In Harmony With Nature: Paintings by Au Ho-nien, by Barry Till, 1985.

Quest for World Peace: Ceramics by Kazuaki Kita, by Barry Till, 1985.

Stencil Prints by Watanabe Sadao, by Barry Till, 1985.

Chinese Jade: Stone for the Emperors, by Barry Till and Paula Swart, 1985.

Arts of the Middle Kingdom: China, by Barry Till and Paula Swart, 1986.

The Legacy of Japanese Printmaking, by Barry Till, 1986.

The Art of Xu Beihong (1895-1953), by Barry Till, 1987.

The Japanese Shinto Shrine at the Art Gallery of Greater Victoria, by Barry Till, 1987.

The Miniature Art of Qu Ru, by Barry Till, 1987.

Figure Painting of the Edo Period (1615-1868), by Barry Till, 1987.

Images from the Tomb: Chinese Burial Figurines, by Barry Till and Paula Swart, 1988.

The Art of Chao Shao-an, A Lingnan Master, by Barry Till, 1988.

Japanese Paintings in the L. Wright Collection, by Barry Till, 1988.

Ceramics of Mainland Southeast Asia, by Barry Till, 1988.

Wonders of Earliest China, by Barry Till, 1989.

Chinese Art from the Rev. Dr. James M. Menzies Family Collection, by Barry Till and Arthur R. Menzies, 1989.

Art From the Roof of the World: Tibet, by Barry Till and Paula Swart, 1989.

Woodblock Prints by Kiyoshi Saito, by Barry Till, 1990.

Relic from a Distant Temple, Victoria's Chinese Bell, by Barry Till, 1992.

The Blue and White Porcelain of China, by Barry Till and Brain S. McElney, 1992.

The Brown Stonewares of the Yixing Kilns, by Barry Till and Paula Swart, 1992.

Hui Jen, by Barry Till, 1992.

Chan Ky-Yut, by Barry Till, 1992.

The Arts of Meiji Japan (1868-1912): Changing Aesthetics, by Barry Till, 1995.

Kesa: The Elegance of Japanese Monks' Robes, by Barry Till and Paula Swart, 1996.

Mandate of Heaven: Treasures from China's Imperial Dynasties, by Barry Till, 1996.

The Gallery Collects/Shin Hanga, by Barry Till, 1996.

Stone slab with relief of rider
(perhaps female general of Yang family)
Ming dynasty (1368–1644)
alabaster; 45.5×42 cm
Private collection

Welcome to
China's Imperial Past